FATAL HEALING

by
Donald E. Whitman

Higher Ground Studios
Lawrenceville, Georgia
U. S. A.

FATAL HEALING

FATAL HEALING
ISBN 0-9754288-8-8

This book is dedicated to Mama,
a truly selfless person,
who always told me I could.

Acknowledgements

I am truly blessed to have a wonderful family – wife, children, brothers, sisters and even in-laws – who have supported me and encouraged me. My wife, Barbara, put up with my questions and frustrations and acted as encourager, editor and quiet mainstay. My brother, Howe, encouraged me to keep going, and his wife, Vicki, and sisters, Marilyn and Tricia, kept me believing in myself. Sister-in-law, Elaine, the English teacher, put up with and encouraged me. My mother-in-law, Henrietta, who has always treated me as one of her own, encouraged me as always. My brother Philip even gave me a six or seven, and Lewis carefully pointed out every misspelling.

And my daughters, Carin and Leslie, made me feel good with their endorsements. Friends, Tim Koby and Ashley Koby acted as sounding boards and cheerleaders, and Stephanie at Higher Ground Studios held my hand the whole way. I love you all, and I hope you enjoy this final version. Thank you for everything, and God Bless You!

-I-

The four conspirators had talked about it at length, a process that inured them to what they were actually doing. It was now acceptable, logical, even a good thing. After all, it would serve the better good. The cure for the common cold - a sickness that had been around since life began, affected people the world over, and sometimes killed the weakest - was at hand. A few hundred or even a thousand lives would be a small price to pay for making it readily available. Surely, even God would not fault them for taking extreme measures to make it available, nor begrudge them the profits they would make. Besides, each, in his own way, had promised a portion of those profits to Him for His assistance in this worthy cause.

It fell to Greg Bolin to introduce balium into the Chinese population. As luck would have it, a scientific seminar was scheduled the next week in Hong Kong, which gave him an easy, and, if ever questioned, a legitimate reason to be there. He spent a fair amount of time trying to figure out the best way to accomplish his task. Balium is a solid, not vapor or gas, but it could be changed to liquid status. The genetically manufactured substance is so potent that even a miniscule amount would be devastating. Once contracted, the sickness would be so contagious, there would be no stopping it without the antidote. But, initially, it must be exposed to people who already had a cold or flu; it did not cause the sickness, it simply enhanced it. A hospital would be one logical place. But how?

In the end, it was really child's play. Greg packed three small vials of balium capsules in his shaving kit and carried it on the plane. He really did not worry about security, because the substance was not metallic or a drug that would be sensed by equipment or dogs. The capsules were ordinary looking, and would easily pass for a prescription drug or even a vitamin. In fact, clearing security at Hartsfield-Jackson International Airport was less strenuous than the mass transit ride he had to take getting there. And clearing Hong Kong customs was just as easy. He could not help but wonder at the futility of most of the security checks implemented since 9/11.

Upon arrival, he checked into his hotel, poured the powder from the capsules into the vials, then walked the short three blocks to Hong Kong Central Hospital, marveling at the street vendors and their unusual wares. It was a beautiful day, and he enjoyed the sights along the way. He entered the hospital without hesitation. A visit to the cafeteria, which he found to be all too similar to hospital cafeterias in the United States, and a palmed dose of balium into the fried rice - the same that would be served to the patients - was really all it took. And he had two vials left.

The Chinese people truly value their elders. A nursing home visit is so common, there are no security measures. Everyone smiled and nodded their heads at the American visitor. Nothing unusual. A good son-in-law, probably. No questions about identity; no questions at all. All facilities were readily available. Another dose to the sweet and sour sauce was simple enough. And he still had one vial left.

Homeless shelters, where they exist, all have something in common. The people are weak and frail for the most part. Many are sick, and few are able to seek medical treatment. It was not really hard to go through the food line; and it was no problem to empty the third vial into the steamed dumplings.

There was some satisfaction, if Greg would face that fact, in knowing those who were initially exposed were at least either already on their deathbed or were, for the most part, already lost to the world. He was not really happy with himself after all was done. Nor was he really upset, as he once thought he would be. He had convinced himself the world would be a better place once the cure was available. This was a small price to pay. In fact, dying in this way would probably be the only way some of these people would ever serve mankind. They had been taking all their lives. It was now their turn to give - even if they were unaware of it.

He was back home in four days. The group met. It would only be a short time now before the first cases started showing up. They each wondered how and when some doctor would ring the bell and pronounce there was a serious problem. It would be hard for someone to take that first step, they knew.

A doctor who yells "wolf" and is proven wrong... well one's reputation has to be protected. A doctor who goes out on a limb and is wrong, might have that limb cut off. On the other hand, the doctor who first diagnoses a new disease would be held in great esteem, and would find himself inundated with new patients. It would be a tough call.

They would see each other in the hall and wonder - is today the day? The first two weeks were almost surreal. "It" had to be happening, but there was no indication it was. No news was certainly not good news right now. They all went through their daily routines and watched the television intently for the first rumblings of a terrible new sickness in China. They did their jobs, went home, exercised, had dates, drank, and just carried on.

They actually missed the first news report. It came three weeks later, and they all knew it was time. But, it was a weekend, and they were doing other things. Actually, they were just bored with waiting. So they missed it. They could not miss the following weeks of reports. All the news stations fought each other for the latest and greatest revelations about the terrible sickness that was sweeping Hong Kong. The disease even received a name - Severe Acute Respiratory Syndrome, or SARS. Researchers searched for a cure as the deaths escalated. The elderly and the weak began dying on a daily basis.

The Chinese government uncharacteristically admitted trying to cover up the magnitude of the epidemic. Some top officials lost their jobs in the ensuing uproar. Whole areas of the population were quarantined. People around the world were television witnesses to a population in distress. Nearly everyone wore the familiar surgical masks. Street vendors selling the masks sprang up along the roads leading from the airport. Generally, people reacted just as Jim Wooten had predicted. Not only did sales of cotton masks soar, the demand for the personal air purification equipment skyrocketed. Stock prices for CONTAC, the fully owned subsidiary of Condor Corporation and the manufacturer of surgical masks and personal air purifiers, reached record levels. And the four men at the top of Condor smiled. For a while.

-2-
Three Weeks Earlier

Bill Horton sat nervously in his chair in front of Jim Wooten's desk. He felt like the messenger who was about to be shot for bringing bad news. The company President was glowering at him even as he finished a phone call.

"Bill, I want you to tell me exactly where we are, and I don't want any more pussy-footing around about it. Now what in the hell is going on?" he asked, after hanging up the phone.

"Mr. Wooten, I really haven't been trying to hide anything. I just hoped the news would get better, and I would not have to bother you...but, it hasn't," the company accountant said.

"Go on."

"Well, as you know, we have spent a ton of money on research on the new drug, REFLEX. We now know that although it does stimulate the production of synovial fluid and cartilage re-growth like we hoped, it has complications that we may not be able to solve." He paused.

"How much have we spent, and what is the problem?" asked Wooten.

Bill cleared his throat. "We've spent more on this drug than any other because the profit potential was so high, and because we kept seeing so much progress. It wasn't until recently that any problem showed up..."

"How much?" a much exasperated Wooten exclaimed.

"Almost two hundred million dollars," Horton whispered. He paused, and then continued when he saw the look on his boss's face. "The drug worked perfectly, but then we started seeing deterioration in the animals that had the earliest treatments. The new cartilage calcified and started causing extreme pain in the joints. In some cases the cartilage actually started crumbling when the joints were forced to move. It's almost like it turns to concrete, it gets so stiff. Gene Windom, who is Greg Bolin's research assistant, wrote it up in the project report. We would have so many lawsuits against us if we put the drug on the market...." His voice trailed off.

Wooten leaned back in the chair rubbing his nose. "I knew we had spent more on this drug than any other. I didn't know it was quite that much, though. What next, can we fix this? And what is the bottom line?" He seemed much calmer now that the truth was out, and Bill lost some of his nervousness.

"The problem may not be able to be fixed. The very ingredients that stimulate synovial fluid also cause the problem. We have to start over. And we can't afford to. Even the big boys can't stand to lose that much money. With our other research projects and with our on-going expenses and overhead, we are not even breaking even. We are staying afloat by, well,

Fatal Healing

by 'creative financing.' But we have to stop the bleeding. We can't put any more money in this project now," he concluded.

James Wooten regarded his accountant balefully. He knew the problem was not Bill's fault. Truth be known, it was more his than anyone else's. But the man was such a wuss, he was an easy target for his frustration. He willfully reigned in his emotions and tried to think analytically. Despite his playboy lifestyle, the company president was a brilliant man, and when the necessity arose, he had always been able to solve complex situations. He prided himself on being able to think clearly and objectively and come up with innovative ideas.

"How are we progressing with COLD-X?" Wooten asked, referring to another drug currently being developed by the company.

Bill hesitated, thrown off guard by the change in subject. "I, well, we... Greg seems pretty positive at the weekly development meetings, but we are still a long way off. The success rate is phenomenal, but we haven't even started our approval process yet. I really don't know exactly how long before we are ready. Our expenses for that project are actually much lower than normal. That's one reason we went ahead and spent the money on REFLEX."

Wooten looked at the accountant and said "I want Bolin and Tim Murray and you to meet with me here at two o'clock. And I want some answers and some ideas. I don't care what else they have planned. You contact them. Two o'clock. Now get out, I have work to do."

♦ ♦ ♦

Greg Bolin, Tim Murray and Bill Horton filed into Jim Wooten's office promptly at two o'clock. Their mood was somber. They were not looking forward to this meeting. But each knew it was a necessity, and each hoped Mr. Wooten could pull another rabbit out of the hat and come up with a quick solution to the financial mire they were in. They all knew that without what Bill Horton called "creative financing," the value of their company stock would be a fraction of what it was trading at now. Each man had weighed his situation carefully during the last year and knew that leaving the company was not really an option. Each had large salaries that would be hard to replicate somewhere else; each had large stock options tied to their longevity with the company, and, most importantly, each had very large outstanding mortgages on their homes. The company had loaned them the money at sweetheart rates, and the loans would immediately be due in full should they leave. Further, each man respected — and feared— Jim Wooten. There was no doubt he was brilliant, but each knew he could be ruthless if crossed, and he never forgot. For better or worse, they were stuck with the company and each other. Hopefully this meeting would generate a solution to their current problem.

"Close the door, Bill," directed Wooten. Bill complied, and the men all took a chair and waited expectantly for their boss to continue. "All right. We all know that we've got problems. Greg, you start by telling us about REFLEX. How bad is it?"

Greg cleared his throat and began. "It is about as bad as it gets. We thought we had the hottest new drug of the century, and now it looks like it is totally useless. Just about every active person develops knee and other joint problems by the time they reach their fifties. This drug would have revolutionized the treatment because it actually stimulates new cartilage growth. However, almost one hundred percent of the new cartilage gets hard and brittle after a few years. We had no way to know that until now"

"Look," interrupted Wooten, "I know that much. What I want to know is can we save it? Is there anything we can add or take away that will solve the problem?"

"Of course we are looking at that, but my feeling is *no*, there isn't. The very chemicals that cause the growth are the same ones that cause the problem. I know we have a tremendous amount of time and money invested in this project, and I am sickened by it, but I think we are pouring good money after bad. I think we should scale research back on this one right now. Sure, let one or two analysts keep looking at altering the chemicals to solve the problem, but let's concentrate on some of our other projects that have a lot more promise, like COLD-X."

Jim Wooten studied his chief scientist thoughtfully. He did not like the message, but he did appreciate they way Greg Bolin delivered the facts without sugar coating them. He knew Greg would tell him the truth, not just what he wanted to hear. He turned to Tim Murray.

"Tim, how many people are assigned to this project? How many will need to be terminated? And how many can realistically be assigned to another area?"

Tim paused, and then said, "There are ten research assistants and another twenty or so support personnel. I think we should leave one or two on it, and move the others to one of our start-up projects. We will be able to fruitfully use them all. We have a couple of drugs in the infant stage that we could use help on."

Bill Horton spoke up. "We have to stop the bleeding on REFLEX, but that's not all. The salaries of these people are significant, but it is the cost of continued research that is killing us. I have crunched the numbers, and even if we stop now and reassign these people, we will show a huge loss this year, and there is no way to cover it, unless we can generate a much larger sales volume on some of our other products. If we have to report that kind of loss, our stock price will plummet."

Wooten was a little surprised his timid accountant had finally put things in perspective and rewarded him with a half-smile, as he turned back to Greg Bolin.

"Give me the short version of where we are on COLD-X, Greg."

"Well, it looks like COLD-X is finally the cure for the common cold. The way it works is to introduce an agent that, if left alone, would actually make the cold far worse, but then COLD-X immediately kills the agent and in so doing, it kills the cold. We have had a 100% success rate in our research, and we are about six months away from applying to the FDA for approval. Unfortunately, even if all goes perfectly, we still won't have the drug approved for several years, so it won't help offset our losses this year. But eventually, it will be a huge money maker."

Fatal Healing

"Tell me more about this agent that "if left alone would make the cold far worse," said Wooten.

"Well, this agent is one that we genetically manufactured in our labs. We call it balium. It acts as a sort of catalyst to the cold and becomes the dominant gene within minutes. COLD-X kills the balium, and the cold simply dies with it. We have introduced the balium into research animals with colds and, when left alone, it would magnify the symptoms of the cold so greatly, they would be near death. It also makes this 'super cold' highly contagious. But within hours of taking the other ingredient of COLD-X, the symptoms start to go away, and within forty-eight hours they are pretty much totally healed. It is really incredible to see. The balium and the 'antidote,' if you will, are in the same capsule. The antidote has a heavier coating, so the balium enters the bloodstream first, takes over the cold, then a short time later the antidote kills it, and the cold is cured. And it is a one shot deal. They take one capsule, and their cold is gone."

Jim Wooten leaned back in his chair and thoughtfully regarded the men. He already knew everything Greg had said about COLD-X; he just wanted confirmation. Now that he had it, he thought he knew a way out of the current financial crises. In fact, done properly, it could be like the goose that laid the golden eggs.

However, the solution was not without risks. If they were caught, no amount of money would keep them out of jail. If they were successful, his company would be seen as a sort of savior of mankind and would reap huge financial rewards. He regarded the men before him and wondered if they would have the fortitude to go along with his plan. He knew their situations as well as they did, and he did not see another way out for them. But if he shared his plan and one or all refused to play ball…it would get very ugly. He really had no choice, he thought. He had never been poor and never intended to be. This would save his company, and nothing else out there could.

"Gentlemen," he began, "I know a way to solve our problem." The three men looked at each other and then at their boss with amazement in their eyes. "However," he continued, "the solution, while easily implemented, is not totally without risk. It would have a disastrous effect on the company and on each of us personally, if we were found out. Jail time would be a certainty. But, as long as each of us keeps quiet, there is virtually no way we would ever be caught. We would all reap millions. I am not going to say any more about it now. I want you to go home and think about it and decide what you are willing to risk. Ya'll sleep on it and be back here at nine-tomorrow morning. And, as always, what is discussed in this room stays in this room."

The men looked at each other and stood up. Without a word they filed out in the same order they entered. No one spoke as each man contemplated the meeting and the unusual turn of events. They knew their boss was brilliant and ruthless when he had to be, but how far would he really go? And how far will I, they each wondered.

◆◆◆

Greg Bolin parked his jaguar XJ12 in the first bay of his four-car garage. The trip home, usually a time of frustration, had been uneventful. If asked, he would not have been able to recall any part of the journey. He had been totally engrossed in thoughts of the day's events and had driven without any thought of the outside world. He obviously had made all the right turns, because he was home. He sat in the car for several more minutes, thinking.

Life had treated him well for the most part. He married his ex-wife, Donna, right after graduation from MIT. They had been lovers for the last two years of college, and it just seemed the proper progression of their relationship. The marriage lasted ten years before they realized they really had very little in common. The union produced no children, and there was nothing to hold them together. The divorce had been amiable, and, for a while, they even kept in touch. Then Donna remarried and started a family. He had not heard from her in seven or eight years.

He had a brother named Philip, who lived on the West Coast, and who he had seen twice in the last five years - once at his mother's funeral, and once at his father's. Both parents had died of congestive heart failure. The brothers had been close growing up but drifted apart during college. They generally talked to each other on holidays and birthdays. Philip was happily married, with three children, so the burden was actually on Greg to go visit, and he had just not done so.

Following his divorce, Greg spent more and more time at Condor, and eventually caught the eye of Jim Wooten. He had been chief research scientist for almost ten years with an income that reflected his success. He liked the good life. His home sat on seven acres and had over 8000 square feet, a four-car garage and a tennis court. He vacationed at least six times a year and liked to gamble. He had several lady friends and enjoyed taking one with him on trips. He owned a nice boat on Lake Lanier, two cars and a truck. He was looking forward to purchasing a retirement home on the West Florida coast.

Greg had over one hundred thousand dollars in the bank and a sizable 401k. But the 401k funds were made up almost entirely of Condor stock, which would be virtually worthless if the company went under. The company held the mortgage to his home, and it would become due if he left for any reason. The hundred grand would not last him a year at his current rate of spending. He wasn't absolutely sure what Wooten had in mind, although he had an idea. It really didn't matter. He was in. No way was he giving up all this.

♦♦♦

Bill Horton sat in the basement of his inner city home and drank. He was alone, as normal. He had never married and did not really enjoy being with women that much. A few flings in college were enough to convince him that sex wasn't all it was cracked up to be, and women were a real pain most of the time. He had never been with a man and did not think he was homosexual, even though he had given it passing consideration from time to time. He was just a loner – a loner who was on his fourth double scotch and was feeling no pain.

Bill was not enamored by very much. Clothes were something to wear, and that was about it. His wardrobe was generally old and tired looking. He purchased new clothes only when those he had wore out. He drove a four year old, four cylinder, automatic Honda Accord for which he paid cash. His one extravagance was his home, which was near Inman Park and had been completely renovated by the previous owner. Bill had seen the house one time and paid the asking price for it one week later with a loan from Condor. He made great money and had made some good investments. He had no family and no debt other than the home, and he could probably pay that off if he needed to.

He did not have a clue what Wooten had in mind. What could he possibly do that would wipe out the debt the company had run up these last two years? He did not know, but he would tomorrow. He was in, too. He had no choice. If the company had to file bankruptcy, the SEC would be investigating, and his "innovative accounting" would be exposed. And he would go to jail. It really isn't innovative to classify over 200 million in bank loans as income so the bottom line looked good to the public. It's just illegal. When he first did it, he thought surely that REFLEX would quickly take off, and the loans would be repaid with no one being the wiser. He knew that Wooten knew what he was doing, but there had never been any discussion of it. There was only one person who would ultimately pay the price if his book cooking were discovered. Him. The way he figured it, if they did nothing, the company would go bankrupt, his shenanigans would be discovered, and he would go to jail. If they followed the boss's plan and got caught, at least he would have company. And if they did not get caught... home free! Oh, I'm definitely in, he thought, as he poured another scotch.

♦♦♦

Tim Murray finished up his four-mile jog with a burst of speed that carried him the last 100 yards. He worked out at least four times a week and was in great shape. He slowed to a walk and cooled down. He normally ran in the early morning before it got so hot. He was flushed and sweat poured down his face, even with the sweatband. The run was a good way for him to think about events of the day and get some exercise, too. He tried to put it all in perspective as he ran. He wished he knew what Wooten had in mind. Was it really bad or just a little on the illegal side of the fence, he wondered for the fifth time. He hoped it was the latter, because he had made his decision. He was in.

Tim was happily married with a daughter and a son. His wife of twenty-five years, Ellen, had worked when they were first married, but Tim's income had allowed her to stay at home after their son was born. Now she did volunteer work and enjoyed spending time around the house. Tim made very good money at Condor, and he was used to it. His children had gone to private schools; they were both in college, and they both had fairly new cars. His home was large and elegant and came with the usual Condor mortgage. He and Ellen owned a two-bedroom condo in Destin, Florida that was almost paid for. They enjoyed taking trips together, and, in general, life was good.

He had fifty or so thousand dollars in savings and a 401k that was close to seven hundred thousand, at today's stock prices. It was entirely Condor stock. If the company went under, so did his plans for retirement. Sure, they could sell the house, move to the condo, and he could get another job. But not one that paid half as much. His kids would have to get student loans. His whole life would change. No way. Tim was not good at change. He ate the same breakfast everyday. He ran the same course every time he jogged. He always bought Grande Marquee cars; he liked his life the way it was. If Jim Wooten had figured out a way to keep things the way they were, and even to make them all millionaires, he was in. Ellen might not understand, and he would not talk to her about it. Let her remain blissfully unaware there was any threat to their way of life.

♦♦♦

Jim Wooten stood on his back deck smoking his daily cigar and looking out over Lake Spivey, a private 600-acre lake in Jonesboro. Only 25 minutes from downtown and 20 minutes from the airport, the lake was surrounded by mini-mansions on one acre plus lots. He had purchased a lot and house for six hundred thousand, then tore the house down and built his home. It was a house built for entertainment. He had divorced his first wife, and then, his trophy wife. Now he shared his home and bed with a fairly steady stream of girls that would have been his daughter's age, had he had children. He knew they were there for the money, and he did not care. He figured it was a fair exchange. He would treat them well, take them on trips, buy them jewelry, and then dismiss them when he tired of their charms.

He watched as a water skier, a wake boarder and a jet ski competed for any vestige of smooth water, even as the sun was setting with a fiery red glow. He loved the lake, even if he rarely used it. He had a two-year-old Ski Nautique with about twenty hours on it, and a twenty-six foot pontoon he used probably twenty times a year - usually at night with one of his girlfriends or with some politico he wanted to impress.

He had been born to money, but in truth, he would have become rich if he had started with nothing. He was brilliant; he was charismatic, and he was not the least bit impressed by rules or laws. He had an innate ability to identify what he wanted and how to get it expeditiously. And nothing, no person or circumstance, was going to change his lifestyle. He knew the plan he had in mind would devastate many lives, perhaps even panic an entire country. He also knew that it would save his company and generate hundreds of millions, if not billions, in profit. He did not need to justify his actions to himself; he understood who he was very well. If he were forced to justify them to someone else, he would explain that much of the money he made would be invested in research for drugs that would benefit mankind, and that, in fact, this plan, while illegal, was actually justified by the end results.

Fatal Healing

He knew there was a risk of being found out and prosecuted. But, like many men who are used to doing things their way without consequence, he figured that with his money and political influence, he was pretty much untouchable. "Ten foot tall and bullet proof," as the song goes. He did not like having to involve the others, simply because of loose lips, but he felt confident he could control them. Also, he mused, if something did go wrong, there would be someone else for him to point to, and he could plead ignorance.

◆◆◆

Jim Wooten knew he had them when they walked into the office. Greg closed the door without being told, and the three men sat and looked expectantly at their boss. He looked at them each briefly and then started without preamble. "I want each of you to know the proposal I have in mind is illegal. We could all go to jail. But I think there is very little risk that we will be found out. If successful, the company will be saved, and I will guarantee each of you a one million dollar bonus. That is in addition to the substantial profits you will see in your stock portfolio. I will not sugarcoat this. I am prepared to go forward only if each of you signs a statement that you are fully aware of what we are doing, that you know it is illegal, and that you have chosen to proceed. I will keep the letters in a safe place and will return them to you with your bonus after we have been successful. If you are not all agreed, I will instruct our attorney to file for bankruptcy protection, and let the chips fall where they may. I have enough investments and money that I will be fine. If it weren't for all of our employees and you, and our stockholders, I would just as soon let it go and then go fishing," he lied.

The three men looked at each other and then back to him.

"I'm in," said Tim Murray,

"Me too" echoed Horton. They all turned and looked expectantly at Greg Bolin.

"I guess I don't understand about the statement. I mean, I don't think this would happen, but what's to keep you from using that against us? And what assurance do we have about the million dollars? I mean right now, we're all in this together, but what if something goes sour down the road?"

There was a nervous silence as all waited for the boss's response. Wooten knew that only Greg would be brave enough to ask the questions, and he was secretly pleased he understood these men so well. He was ready with the answers.

"First off, these statements are to protect ME from YOU, if things go 'sour,' as you put it. I am the president of this company, and I will be the one who catches the most scrutiny. No way could something go wrong, and I not catch the blame. And I'm not taking chances that one of you might want to cut your own deal by pleading ignorance. Further, I couldn't very well use the statements against you without further implicating myself. Second off, while I have the most to gain if everything works out, I also have the most to lose if they don't, so you can bet on me being in for the duration. And third, if everything goes right, and I think it will, there will be plenty of money. I would be an idiot to try to renege on the top three officers in the company and take a chance on losing everything. Greg, I may be a lot of things, but I am not guilty of being an idiot. Now, in or out?"

Greg took about two seconds to consider what was said. "You are right, of course. I'm in. Let's sign the statements and then hear about our salvation."

Wooten already had the statements prepared. The men each looked at their statement briefly and signed without comment. They handed the signed agreements back to their boss. He turned his back on them, and opened a fireproof and heavy-duty floor safe. He locked up the documents and then turned to the men and smiled.

"The plan is really quite simple. We will introduce balium into a densely populated foreign country, like China. In fact, China is perfect. There are plenty of people, and there is plenty of money. The severe cold symptoms will spread rapidly, because it is so contagious. The ailment will reach epidemic proportions, and there will be panic. Tourism will come to a halt. A large portion of the work force will be either too sick or too scared to go to work. Government services will come to a virtual stand still. The population will be in total turmoil. Hospitals and doctors will be overwhelmed. There will be mass quarantines to try and stop the spread. But, that won't work either. The powers that be will be frantic to find a cure or treatment. Sales of our surgical masks and personal air purifiers will explode. The profits generated from that alone will keep us in the black. We'll ride that wave for a while, and when the time is right, we will introduce the antidote. It will work quickly and completely. The demand will be tremendous. The government won't give a rat's ass about extended trials and testing. After all, what could be worse than the disease? Sales will be off the chart. Meanwhile, it is inevitable the sickness will spread to other countries. England, Canada, here. Our government will look at the antidote's success where it has been used, and the FDA will bend all the rules so that we can immediately make the cure available. We will be rich and heroes, as well. Our biggest problem will be keeping up with the demand."

There was stunned silence as the men all looked at their boss. Tim Murray broke the silence. "But, I mean, you can't be serious! People will die! Families will be ruined."

Wooten stopped him "Wait a minute. Did you think that a solution to our problem - a quick way to makes hundreds of millions would be simple, would be without consequence, and would be without risk? Yes, people will die. That's what causes the panic. But people die every day. Over there, over here, everywhere. And the people that die will be the old and the weak - the very same type of people that will benefit the most when our cure for the common cold is available. Eventually, more will be saved than will actually die. Now I think that is a good thing. And if any of you has a better idea, let's hear it." Not a sound was heard.

Greg Bolin left for China the following week to attend the medical conference being held there. He was carrying balium.

-3-

All was well at the Condor Pharmaceutical Corporation. The SARS virus had caused sales of CONTACT products to soar, and the company's stock prices were up. Everyone's 401k was doing well. Morale was high. All was as it should be. Everyone was happy. Almost.

Gene Windom was a research assistant at Condor. Not just anyone's assistant, though. He was Greg Bolin's chief assistant and worked exclusively for him. For the past three years he had worked continually on Cold-X. He was excited about his job and the prospects of this new drug. It was he who had initially formulated balium; he who was intimately familiar with how it worked, and what it did; and it was he who knew something was not quite right about the SARS epidemic. As his daddy used to say, " I may have been born in the dark, but it wasn't last night," he thought now as he drank beer and watched the latest news about SARS. Gene was far from dumb, and it did not take a mental giant to put it all together. Greg Bolin decides on the spur of the moment to take his place at the science convention in Hong Kong. A month after his return all hell breaks loose with this SARS thing. The symptoms are exactly like those balium would cause. And the company's stock was climbing like a rocket. He was happy to see the value of his 401k increasing like everyone else, but that was not enough. He felt like there was a big party, and he had not been invited.

He was pretty sure he knew how the epidemic started, and had a good idea of why. But there were two things he could not figure out. First, why like this - taking a chance like this. The drug would be approved in a couple of years anyway. And no laws would be broken. No one would die. He knew that Bolin was not hurting for money, so what was it? The second question was the one he spent the most time with. How could he best cash in on it?

Gene was forty-three years old, divorced and the proud parent of two daughters with whom he spent every other weekend and every special occasion he could. He was short and slender, with slightly balding brown hair and brown eyes. He was generally quiet and even gave the appearance of being shy. During high school and college he had been the typical nerd. He was involved in academic pursuits and little else. His success at Condor had given him the confidence he needed, and he was a much more rounded person now.

He and his ex-wife, Sheila, had gone their separate ways two years earlier. The divorce had not been without acrimony, but it had not been particularly vicious. Now they each made a concerted effort to not undermine the other with the children. Neither he nor his ex had re-married and they were glad to share custody. Frankly, each was happy for a few nights and

Fatal Healing

weekends out. They loved their children, but they each wanted at least some semblance of a life of their own. It just worked out better for them to get along. Bill always paid his child support on time, and was proud to do so. He wanted to support his children, and would have even without the court order that made it a necessity. It did, however, put a financial strain on him. House mortgage, insurance, child support, utilities and food expenses left very little for pleasure. But now....

Gene never played the lottery, but he had the feeling he had just won one! Like all big lottery winners, he worried about how and when to cash in his winning ticket. He wrestled with that problem for several days, and finally decided he would approach his boss first thing in the morning and just tell him what he knew, then play it by ear. He went through every scenario he could think of, and they all ended with him getting lots and lots of cash. Enough that his children would no longer have to go to public school, and he would be able to do anything he wanted. Sometimes he even thought about how Sheila would want to get back together, once she knew he had obviously received a huge promotion. These thoughts were usually quickly replaced with ones of how she would react to the beautiful young ladies he would now be able to squire.

Approaching his boss like that would be a bold step for Gene, almost totally out of character. But he was sure of himself about this matter, and he felt emboldened by his knowledge. His knowledge gave him power, a foreign feeling for him, but one he found very pleasing.

♦♦♦

Bolin usually arrived in the office around nine a.m., and the next morning was no exception. He spoke to Jim Billups, the security guard, as he entered the main foyer of the building and proceeded to the elevators. Using his security card he rode the elevator to his floor. RESEARCH was printed boldly on the lone door in the hall. He used his card again to open this door and entered into another short hallway and door. To the left of this door was what appeared to be a cross between an old fashioned camera and a pair of binoculars, with a plastic chin cup. In order to enter this door and the "inner sanctum" as he called it, he first had to put his chin in the cup and look into the retina scanner. As the machine recognized his retina, there was a barely audible click and the door opened on its own.

Greg walked past the rows of cubicles, speaking to the occasional person already at work. He entered his office and turned on the light. His office certainly did not match the splendor of the company president's, but it was large and well appointed. A corner office, it had a view of the parking lot out one window and a view of well-landscaped company grounds out the other. Greg crossed the floor, put his briefcase on the desk and used the remote control to turn on the television for the morning news. He went back to the hallway and walked down to the employee break room to get coffee. Returning to his office, he sat at his desk drinking coffee and catching the morning news, reading <u>The Atlanta Journal</u> during advertisements. He quickly tired of local news channels, with their local news stories anchored by traffic and weather every ten minutes. He switched to Channel 37 - FOX News, and listened while the talking head, in this case an attractive blonde of about thirty, gave an update on SARS. Two more people had died over the weekend, and the panic showed no signs of abatement.

Gene Windom walked past the still unoccupied secretary's desk and knocked on the door to his boss's office. He opened the door and stuck his head in.

"Can I talk to you a minute?" he asked.

Bolin looked up, surprised. It was not unusual for his chief research analyst to need a little of his time, but it was unusual for him to enter like this, without an appointment.

"Come in, Gene, what's the problem?"

Gene walked across the room and chose the center chair of the three facing his boss's desk. He looked at Bolin, then at the TV, which now showed a picture of rush hour pedestrian traffic in China. Everyone, it seemed, was wearing the familiar surgical masks. He looked back at Bolin and nodded toward the TV.

"How much longer are you going to let that go on?" he asked.

Bolin looked at the TV and back at Gene. "What do you mean?"

"I mean, how much longer before you let them know we have the cure for that? How much longer before you tell them about COLD-X? I imagine the Chinese government would wave at normal procedures and put the drug to immediate use." He paused. "That is the plan, isn't it?"

Bolin could feel his face turning red as he stared at his associate. "I think you better explain yourself. And be very careful of any accusations you make," he said coldly.

Gene had only a moment's doubt about his conclusions. But he had thought this out too carefully, and he was sure he was right. His voice was calm as he started again.

"Look, Greg, don't forget that I know the effects of balium better than anyone on earth. I formulated it, worked with it and have studied it for two years, now. You take my place at the conference in Hong Kong and shortly after you return, SARS hits. Now don't get me wrong. I'm not complaining. My 401k has really started humming now that our stock prices are up, and I really don't care about a bunch of Chinese people. But let's just say that I would like to come to the party, not just get a few snacks as part of the clean-up crew."

Bolin was stunned. A full thirty seconds passed before he spoke. "You have been working too hard. That or you have lost your mind. That is the craziest thing I have ever heard of. You are talking about murder. I can't believe that you think I would be involved in something like that. That is insane! Yeah, there are some similarities to this sickness and what balium causes. But similarities won't cut it, and if it's not exactly the same, then COLD-X would not work. Now get the hell out of my office. Better yet, get the hell off the property. Take a week off and get some rest. You obviously need it. And I will expect an apology when you return." Deny, deny, deny had served him well in the past. It was all he could think to do now.

"Wait a minute, Greg. Like I said, I'm not complaining. I think it's brilliant, I just..." Gene's voice trailed off as his boss stood up.

"I said leave. Now, you can either get up and walk out of here, take a week off and come back to a job, or I will have you escorted off the premises, and you will never work here again." Bolin said angrily. "You have about one second to decide."

The two men stared at each other, and it was Gene who blinked. He got up, started to say something else and thought better of it. He turned and quickly left.

Gene exited the building, got into his late model Toyota and looked up at the building as he put the car in reverse. Bolin was standing at his window watching. Gene exited the property and started home. His mind whirled as he traveled out Camp Creek Parkway towards I-20. This was not the outcome he had dreamed of and planned for. Could he have been wrong? Had he just jeopardized a wonderful job and a promising future for nothing? He went over the facts again and again as he drove home. His mind replayed the conversation in Bolin's office time after time. Where had he screwed up, and what now?

Greg Bolin watched Windom's Toyota drive through the gates and felt a nervous knot in his stomach. He turned to the phone to call Jim Wooten and then realized it would be another hour, at least, before the company president arrived. Of the four who knew, only Bill Horton might be here. But he did not want to talk to the accountant about this. Better to wait for Wooten to arrive and all four get together to talk at the same time. He got another cup of coffee and drank without tasting the liquid, while he considered this turn of events. He knew he could do no work, so he alternately read the paper, watched the news, and looked at his watch as he waited.

He was standing at the window when Wooten's car pulled through the gates. Finally. Like Gene Windom, he too, had gone over the conversation again and again. It did not get any prettier with time. Gene knew. And he should have anticipated he would. He should have known that Gene would figure it out. After all, he was a brilliant man. That's why he worked here. That's why he is so valuable. And that's why he is such a liability. What to do now? Maybe it would be best to bring him into the loop. After all, it appeared that Gene only wanted money. He said he didn't have a problem with the plan. So he just wanted money. He watched Wooten enter the building and started out to intercept him.

-4-

Jim Wooten had awakened early that morning and was eating breakfast and sipping coffee while watching two early morning water skiers take turns running the slalom course. He looked at his watch and realized it was only six-thirty. Hard to believe that people had enough energy to actually get up and go skiing that early. These same guys were out there several times a week, generally going back and forth through the course, but sometimes just skiing the whole lake. Every now and then there was a good-looking blonde with them, but not today. He guessed they skied the course until it got too rough, then skied the lake while the water smoothed out. One guy looked like an aging hippy, with long gray hair. The other, much younger and better-looking, but with less hair, was by far the better skier. Both appeared to be in much better physical condition than he was. The Ski Nautique flashed by on the way down the lake. He sighed, put out his cigarette and went to get dressed for work.

Traffic was light as he traveled toward the office. It had taken him just five minutes to travel from his house up Spivey Road to Hwy 138 and to the interstate. I-75 traffic flowed smoothly, and he had plenty of time to think. Things were going precisely as he had planned. The stock market was up and shares of Condor Corporation were soaring. The SARS epidemic was spreading, with reports of it now in Canada. It would not be too much longer before they introduced the cure. Not long before they would "test" the drug on some critically ill patients, who would then be cured. The Chinese Government would insist on making the drug immediately available. He would reluctantly go along because the disease was so devastating. By then Canada and the United States as well would be looking for the drug's rapid approval. He smiled as he turned into the gated entrance of Condor Corporation. Life was good. He looked at his watch. Thirty-five minutes, door to door. Not bad.

He passed through the guarded gates and parked his car in its reserved spot closest to the building entrance. As he exited the car, he was struck by the humid Georgia heat and knew this day was going to be what the locals called a "scorcher." It was going to be beautiful, clear and sunny. He decided to call a few friends and set up a round of golf for after lunch.

He entered the building, greeted the receptionist and security guard and headed for the elevators. The stainless steel machine did not care if he was the boss, and he had to swipe his security card for it to work. He arrived at his floor and his exuberant mood was shattered as he exited the elevator to face a grim Greg Bolin.

Fatal Healing

"We need to talk," said Greg. Wooten nodded and walked him towards his offices, pausing for two seconds to pick up a small stack of messages offered to him by his secretary.

They entered the office, and Wooten closed the door, motioning Greg towards a chair.

"What is going on?" he asked, as he sat down behind his huge desk.

"We've got a problem. Gene Windom knows what is going on. He was basically waiting for me this morning. He asked how long before we offered the cure. He figured out that balium was causing the problem, and that I had taken his place in Hong Kong...he just figured it out."

Greg's normally unflappable manner had crumbled, and he was now visibly shaken. "We should have figured he would, since he knows so much about the research," he continued.

"Wait a minute, Greg. Slow down. What exactly did he say? What does he want?"

Greg relayed the conversation verbatim and Wooten's mouth twitched when he got to the part about his research chief wanting to "come to the party, not just get some scraps".

Wooten picked up the phone and dialed Tim Murray.

"Get Horton and come to my office. We have a situation. Greg is already here."

He swiveled his chair away from Greg and watched the bank of televisions. The only sound in the room was the barely audible voices of news anchors discussing the terrible sickness spreading across China. The men, both lost in their own thoughts, did not speak again for the entire ten minutes it took for Bill Horton and Tim Murray to arrive.

The voice of Wooten's secretary came out of the small intercom on the desk, as she announced the arrival of the two men. Wooten punched the talk button, and gave the okay for their entrance. They came in and quickly took seats, without being told, and looked expectantly at their boss.

"Tell them, Greg," Wooten said.

Greg started at the beginning and told the men the entire conversation. His demeanor was once again calm, now that some time had passed for him to collect himself. There were no happy faces, as he finished the brief recitation. Bill Horton was the first to speak.

"How could you have missed knowing that Windom would identify the cause of this?" he asked accusingly.

"Hey, wait, you missed it, too. We all did. We just didn't think about a research assistant figuring it out," retorted Greg.

"Yeah, well he works for you, not any of us. I know that none of my people know," was the quick reply.

"Okay, that's enough, guys. This is not doing any good." Wooten interrupted. "Let's figure out how we need to handle this," he continued. "Greg, what do you suggest? You know him better than any of us. What does he want? How dangerous is he?"

Everyone turned to Greg, who thought for a moment before he responded. "Well, he was smart enough to figure it out and brave enough to confront me. I would have to say, he probably thinks he has enough information to collect a lot of money, and that is what motivates him. He has never struck me as being vindictive or anything like that. I would suspect he probably is having some doubts right now, just because I sent him home. But he didn't act rashly this morning. He had given it a lot of thought. He will think about it more and have the same conclusion. I think we are going to have to pay him, probably bring him into the group."

They all turned back to Wooten for his response.

Wooten pulled at his left ear lobe and regarded the men for a moment. "I guess that when you say 'we,' you are talking about all of us, right? So that means we all ante-up equally. If he says it will take one million to keep quiet, we each put up a quarter of a million."

He knew from the look on their faces that was not what they had in mind. "We" was really Condor to them. And that means "me," he thought to himself. The men looked at each other.

Finally, Greg spoke. "I guess that if we bring him in as part of the group, he'll be willing to wait like the rest of us, and we can pay our portion when we get paid," he said quietly.

Wooten sighed audibly and said: "Ya'll get out and think about this. We probably have a couple of days since Greg sent him home. But I doubt he stays gone a week. He smells money, and he is going to want to be fed real soon. We'll get together day after tomorrow at this same time."

The men looked at each other, rose, and filed meekly out.

Wooten turned his back to them as they left and regarded the pictures behind his desk as if they would impart great wisdom. What a bunch of idiots. There was no incentive for Windom to join the group, even if they let him. He just wanted cash. He was clean. He had broken no laws, and he could call the shots. No way would he sign the agreement the others had. And that meant he could keep coming back to the plate every time he got short of cash. It was a "no win" situation as far as he was concerned. That meant the situation had to be changed. He thought for a few more minutes, mulling over his various options. His decision made, he paged his secretary.

"Please get in touch with Slaton and tell him I need to see him right away."

◆◆◆

Rex Slaton was Condor's chief of security. He was a Vietnam veteran who had signed up for three tours there. He found he enjoyed the fighting and was very much at home in the structured military environment. After his discharge he had become an Atlanta policeman. He was with the force over ten years and during that time had several complaints of unnecessary force filed against him. The last had been when a young black man had been beaten to the point of a coma. There was ample evidence the man had resisted arrest, and he was armed with a knife. However, the resulting publicity, along with the previous complaints against him, derailed his police career. Young, with no work experience other than the military and police, and with a stigma attached to him because of all the publicity, Slaton was virtually unemployable. Wooten had rescued him from that, and in return, he had Slaton's unquestioned loyalty.

To Slaton, Mr. Wooten was pretty close to a god. He had not only hired him as chief of security at a salary that was far more than he made as a policeman, he had let the company loan him the money for his house and had given him annual stock bonuses that were now worth a fair amount, especially since stock prices had started climbing. It was fair to say that Wooten and company owned Slaton, and that bothered Slaton not in the least. There was nothing he would not do for the man, and they both knew it.

Slaton was at his desk, reviewing security reports from the previous weekend, when the call came. He hurriedly put away the reports, grabbed his jacket and headed out, smiling. He enjoyed the times he got to meet with the boss. He was a good man. He did not know what this was about, but everything was going well in his department, so he was not worried. He swiped his security card at the elevator and regarded his reflection on the polished steel doors. He was a rather small man, standing about five foot seven inches tall and weighing only one hundred and fifty pounds. The stubble of his shaved head was dark, almost black. He had a prominent nose that had obviously been broken at least once. His arms were longer than normal and were well muscled and sinewy, with prominent blue veins. His brown eyes were close together and were accentuated by heavy dark eyebrows. His uniform was starched and his overall appearance was of a tough, intelligence officer.

He smiled at his reflection as the elevator door shut, and headed to see his benefactor.

Rex Slaton waited while Mr. Wooten's secretary announced his arrival. He looked around, and was again impressed by the luxury of his boss's suite of offices. After receiving approval, he entered Wooten's office.

"Good morning, Rex. Come on in and have a seat."

"Yessir," he replied so quickly that it was all one word.

"How have you been?"

"Fine, sir. Thanks for asking."

"And how is your family? How is Alice?"

"Oh, sir, she is great," replied Slaton, thrilled his boss remembered his wife's name. "And Greg is a senior this year. We are hoping he gets a football scholarship to Georgia. He is small like me, but that boy is so fast..." Slaton stopped and regarded his boss respectfully. He knew this meeting was not about his family.

Wooten leaned forward from his chair. "That's great, Rex. I know you are proud of him." He paused, then said, "Rex, I've got a problem that I hope you can help me with."

"Yes sir. I'll do anything you want. What is it?"

Wooten smiled appreciatively and continued. "We have a problem employee. He has taken secret, sensitive information home. It is about a new drug that we are developing that is almost ready. It will put our company on the map. Now, he is trying to blackmail me, wanting me to pay to get the information back before he sells it to our competitors."

"Who is he?", interrupted Slaton angrily. He could not believe that someone would do that to his boss and his company. "I'll take care of it."

"Well, his name is Gene Windom, Greg Bolin's chief assistant. But how are you going to take care of it?"

Rex thought for a minute and said, "Well, there are a number of things that we could do, but the easiest is that I'll just go to his house with the police and get the information back, then we can have him arrested, or just fire him."

Even as he said it, Rex knew that was too simple. "No, I know," he held up his hand as Wooten started to speak. "That can't work. We don't know where he has the information, and without it we have no proof he has done anything wrong."

"Exactly," said Wooten.

Wooten watched his Chief of security as he weighed different options.

After several minutes Rex looked at his boss and said, "I'm gonna have to do this one on one. Force him to give it up and to tell us whom he has contacted."

"How would you do that? He is no longer at work. He went home this morning."

"I'll have to go to his house, then"

"If you do that, he'll just call the police, and then you will be in trouble again, and we won't have accomplished anything but making him mad."

Slaton thought for a minute. "I don't think he would call the cops. Generally, someone up to no good doesn't want anything to do with the law. But I'll go at night, break in and catch him by surprise, before he can call the cops, even if he wanted to"

This is going exactly as I want, Wooten thought. "Rex, I can't ask you to do that. It is against the law, and you could be arrested. Hell, you could be killed. He probably has a gun."

"Mr. Wooten, if you have a better idea, I will be happy to try it. But I can't think of another way. I'm not worried about getting caught. I was a cop for ten years, remember. I know how to do it. And I'm not that worried about him having a gun. I have one too, and I know how to use it. You and this company have been too good to me. As chief of security, it is my job to protect this company. Don't worry. I can handle this. The way I look at it, he has broken the law, and he is threatening us. We have a right to protect ourselves."

"Well, that's not our only problem. He probably has the information stored on a compact disk. He could give it to us and have another copy he could sell and then, just be gone. Somehow, we have to make sure he can't do that."

"Don't worry about it, Mr. Wooten, I will handle this," he said again. "You don't need to be involved." The two men looked at each other. Neither man verbalized what they each knew was to happen. Wooten stood up, signaling the end of the meeting. He extended his hand to the security officer.

"Thanks, Rex. I knew that I could depend on you to solve something that threatened this company. You are a good man. And don't worry about whether your son gets that football scholarship. If you take care of this problem, he has a full scholarship from us." Rex shook his boss's hand and had tears in his eyes. Wooten was truly a great man, and he was proud to be able to help out after all he had done for him. This Windom guy was going to regret trying to blackmail Condor. He walked back to his office. He was not the brightest light in the sky, but he was cunning, and right now, his mind was working overtime.

-5-

Gene Windom sat on the couch in the family room of his home. The room was large and spacious, with vaulted ceilings and a rock fireplace. It was clean and neat, with everything in its place except for a sit-and-spin toy belonging to his daughters. Gene did not notice any of this, however. He was lost in thought, reliving the scene in Greg Bolin's office. That meeting had turned out all wrong. He had played out all the possible scenarios in his mind, but not this one. Could he have been wrong? Could this have been some outrageous coincidence? He doodled on a pad, writing down the characteristics of the sickness balium would cause and those of SARS. He was not wrong. He knew it with unquestioned certainty. But, he had surely been wrong about Greg Bolin's reaction.

The real question was "What now?" If he stayed home like Bolin had said, it would show he was unsure and be a sign of weakness that Bolin would use. But if he went back now, he had no doubt that security would be called to remove him. He went over Bolin's words and actions time and again. Gradually, it dawned on him that Bolin was stalling for time. Time to talk the situation over with Mr. Wooten and any others who were involved. Of course. He should have anticipated that. Bolin could not handle this without talking to them. And once he did, the inevitable conclusion would be they must have a new partner. He was still in the money. He still had the knowledge.

Normally, Gene was not a very heavy drinker. But it felt like celebration time. He poured himself a scotch and water and smiled. What was that saying? "It is five o'clock somewhere."

Gene woke up from a brief nap, probably induced by the four scotch and waters he had consumed. He fixed some lunch, and then, feeling the need for activity, he mowed the lawn. The lot was heavily wooded, with very little grass, so this task did not take long. He washed the car. He straightened up the house. He piddled. About five o'clock he drove to Blockbuster and rented a movie. He stopped at the grocery store and picked up a steak. He intended to have a quiet night at home. A good meal, a good movie, some more scotch. Tomorrow would be a big day!

♦♦♦

Rex left Wooten's office and went straight back to his own. He ignored the security reports on his desk, setting them into a pile on the floor. He turned to his computer and entered his access code. He pulled up the personnel files and closely examined the information it contained about Gene Windom. There was nothing there to indicate the man would be a security risk. He had graduated top of his class from MIT. Married and had two daughters, then divorced. There was no police record. No sign of habits like gambling that would lead a man to try extortion. On paper, he was ideal. "Oh, that it was so," thought the security chief. "This man has stolen protected information from the company and is trying to blackmail us. He deserves whatever happens," he reminded himself.

He jotted down Windom's address and decided he would drive by and check out the house. It was in Douglas County in a subdivision off River Forest Parkway. He knew the area and did not consult a map. Rex's car was a maroon Toyota Camry several weeks past its last wash. The windows had been tinted, and it was hard for anyone to look into the vehicle. It was a common, non-descript car that drew no attention.

The subdivision was like so many others that dotted the landscape. Large, all vinyl siding with a two-car garage, a small porch, and at least ten more homes just like it scattered about the neighborhood. At least this builder had left the majority of trees instead of scalping the lots like many did. That was probably part of his zoning. This area did not have sewer availability, so the houses were all on septic tank. This meant the lots had to be at least three quarters of an acre. These houses all appeared to be on at least a full acre. Windom lived on a cul-de-sac, and as Slaton turned around, he could see someone he recognized as Windom cutting the grass close to the house and barely visible through the trees. "Talk to you later," he thought, as he drove away and headed to his house, also in Douglasville and less than 15 miles away.

Slaton turned into his driveway and parked in the garage. His son was not home yet, and his wife was at work, so there was no need to enter the house. Instead, he pulled down the attic stairs in the garage and went into the attic area. After removing a one by six floorboard from the right corner of the attic, he retrieved a handgun wrapped in oilcloth. He did not bother to unwrap the gun. He carried it downstairs, shut the attic and was on the way out of his driveway less than five minutes after his arrival. The pistol was a snub nosed .38, just like the one he carried in his job. However, this one had once belonged to a drug dealer who had filed off the serial number. It had not been shot in many years, and so Slaton continued on I-20 West past the town of Villa Rica to a secluded area that was often used for target practice. He came here at least once a month to practice with his service pistol, so no one would take notice of him coming today.

After parking, he unwrapped the gun and checked its movement and firing pin. He loaded the revolver with five 38-caliber shells and carried it and the box of bullets with him. He shot for about five minutes and was very pleased with the gun and his marksmanship. The place was deserted, so he took his time wiping the gun clean and wrapping it in a fresh dry cloth before leaving. There was nothing to do now but wait.

He had been here before. He remembered the feeling. The waiting period before the action that was inevitable. It wasn't really a bad thing, in fact, he had kind of missed it. He could feel the excitement building and just relaxed and enjoyed it.

Fatal Healing

♦♦♦

Jim Wooten stayed in his office for several hours after his security chief left, making calls and trying to catch up on some messages that needed his attention. But his thoughts were never far from the situation at hand. He was taking a risk, he knew, having Rex Slaton go to Windom's house. But not sending him was a risk too, because it was a certainty that Windom would not just go away. And what he knew could put them all in jail. And he would still know it next year and the next and the next, and still be cashing in on it, if left alone. He had no doubt that either Rex Slaton or Gene Windom would die tonight. He was betting his security chief, a Vietnam vet and ex-police officer with extensive training, would be the one left standing. But, Wooten realized, Windom knew his house, and Slaton did not. That would certainly be advantageous to Windom. And if Windom were left standing, then Slaton would certainly be tied back to Wooten. Windom would either sing like a bird or increase his demands. Wooten was nervous. He was not used to being vulnerable, and it was not a pleasant feeling.

♦♦♦

Slaton returned to his home, where he surprised his wife, Alice, who turned into the drive almost at the same time, because he was home so early. He explained he would need to go back to the office later to check up on the night shift. He generally did this two or three times a year, so it was not unexpected. Since he was home early, his wife and son persuaded him to go to eat at their favorite Mexican restaurant.

Slaton was never a big eater, and tonight even less so. He settled for a *Crazy Taco* and one beer, forcing himself to talk to his family and ask about their day. His mind, however, was on what he must do tonight. His wife noticed he was unusually quiet and assumed he was simply thinking about going back to the office, and what he had to do there.

It was almost 11 pm when Gene Windom decided it was time for bed. He felt a little stuffed, having eaten a big steak, baked potato and salad. Then some microwave popcorn and several more scotch and waters, while he watched most of the movie he had rented. When he realized he could not recall what had happened during the last ten minutes of the movie, he gave up and headed for bed. He was asleep in his big king-size bed in less than thirty minutes.

If Windom had purchased the golden retriever his daughters had been begging him to, it might have been different. Rex Slaton had seen the lights go out on his first pass through the neighborhood. He then went back to his office so he could be seen there. He left the office about two. He figured, correctly, that Windom would be sound asleep. He turned into his driveway, without headlights and drove up to the garage area. If Windom was awake for some reason, he would simply say he was checking up on him since he had not been at work and was not on vacation. A flimsy excuse, but a man who was blackmailing the company could hardly call the cops. There was dead silence, and no lights. He went to the front door, pulled out a small compass and ran it down the side of the door, locating the magnet going to the security system. He then quickly picked the lock and held a powerful magnet against the doorframe next to where he had located the magnet in the door. He knew from his many hours of police/security work that the magnet located in the door closed the circuit of the sensor located in the doorframe. His magnet simply replaced the magnet that was in the door, as it swung open. The sensor remained closed and the security system was circumvented. He took a piece of duct tape he had pre-cut for the task and used it to hold the magnet in place. The entire operation took less than two minutes.

Slaton moved quickly into the shadows and waited silently, listening intently for any sound that would indicate someone was awake. Hearing nothing, he walked towards the end of the house where he thought the master bedroom was. His eyes had adjusted to the darkness of the house, and he could now see fairly clearly from the light of the moon outside. He entered the first room he came to, which turned out to be a home office instead of the master bedroom. He started towards the computer, remembering what his boss had said about the information probably being on a disk, then changed his mind and went in search of Windom. He went back through the entrance area to the other end of the house.

He passed the door to the garage and one that appeared to be to a half-bath, and entered the master bedroom. Windom was sleeping on his back in the king sized bed. Slaton took a powerful flashlight from his pocket and shown it directly at

Windom's eyes, from about four feet away. The sleeping man awoke abruptly, reflexively shielding his eyes with his hand.

"Get up, Windom. We've got things to talk about. You are pretty stupid to think you could blackmail us and get away with it. Move very slowly and maybe you won't get hurt."

Windom, still groggy from sleep and alcohol, did not move as his mind tried to come to grips with the situation. Realization can be a brutal thing. When it came to Windom, he felt physically sick. He knew he had tried to play with the big boys and had lost. He did not have any idea what the man behind the light wanted to talk about, but he was certain the part about not being hurt was crap. He flipped the covers back and slowly turned to get out of the bed. He had a gun in the bedside table drawer and thought briefly about getting it, but realized he would not stand a chance. What he needed to do was to create a distraction. That was his only chance.

Windom had purchased this home only three years earlier, after his divorce. The young couple he purchased it from had contracted with the builder to build the house and had installed a panic button on the wall going from the bedroom to the master bathroom. They had shown him this feature when he was looking at the house, but he had never given it any more thought until now. It was easily ignored, because it was just like any other wall switch, except it was a button. Following Slaton's instructions, he slowly rose from the bed and put one hand on the wall, as if to steady himself.

When he pushed the button, the alarm siren pierced the silent night. Even Windom, who knew it was coming, was surprised at the high-pitched siren. He quickly opened the drawer and grabbed the gun and fell to the floor. He fumbled with the gun for a split second and pointed it towards the light. There were three quick gunshots. Windom never knew what hit him. He was dead before his head hit the floor.

Cursing, Slaton ran back through the house to the office and grabbed all the floppy discs in plain sight and fled the house. He pulled off the duct tape and magnet as he left. He could see lights being turned on in the neighbor's house as he drove quickly out of the subdivision. He was two miles and several roads away before his heart slowed down.

"Damn!" he said out loud. "Just Damn."

He was driving on a deserted two-lane road that he had decided upon earlier in the day, because it was in an undeveloped area. He pulled over to the side as he approached a bridge crossing the Flint River. He turned on the interior light. If a car happened by, it would appear he was just looking at a map. No one could see in through the tinted glass. He reached under the seat and grabbed a bag he had placed there that afternoon. He removed a balloon, string, and a swizzle stick. He blew up the balloon, inserted the swizzle stick in the opening and tied it off with string. He then tied the pistol he had just used to the other end of the string. He turned off the light and let down his window. Driving on the left side of the bridge, he tossed the gun with balloon attached over the rail. The swizzle stick would let the air out of the balloon slowly as the current carried it down stream, away from the bridge. If anyone ever looked for it here, they were out of luck. He was not overly concerned. The gun could not be tied to him anyway. He had carefully wiped it down earlier today with alcohol, removing any signs of fingerprints, and had not handled it without gloves since. But, he was taking no chances.

Slaton drove home and took a long hot shower. He let the hot water pound tight muscles as he tried to relax. Shower finished, he put on pajamas and walked through the bedroom, careful not to wake his sleeping wife. He poured himself a strong bourbon and sat in his easy chair trying to unwind. Tonight had not gone as planned. He did not regret killing Windom; he had known that would have to happen. He had not killed anyone since his days in Vietnam. But if he were honest with himself, he would admit to feeling a certain sense of superiority. He had been challenged, and he had won again. Just like Nam.

But he had not had time to question Windom. He did not know if he had retrieved the information that his boss wanted. He had about fifteen discs in a cloth bag he would give to Mr. Wooten tomorrow. Even if he had not retrieved the information, he had at least stopped Windom from using it, he reasoned. He hoped that Mr. Wooten would be happy. He finished his drink and went to bed.

-6-

Debra Raines wheeled thru the guarded gates of the Condor Corporation in her new Miata convertible. She could hardly believe her good fortune. She had just graduated with a master's degree in biology from Tennessee State, and only six months earlier had planned to teach biology. Then came the recruitment offer from Condor. At a salary twice that which she had anticipated as a teacher, and more benefits as well, she was on top of the world. The Miata had been her present to herself to celebrate her good fortune. She parked and unwound herself from the sports car to the bemusement of those watching. At five foot eleven inches she was tall, and it seemed her legs could not possibly fit in that compact area. She accomplished the task gracefully, as would be expected of someone with her athletic prowess. In college she had been on the track team, run hurdles and was the point on the basketball team. Her hair, which until now had been contained by the scarf she wore when the top was down, proved to be about shoulder length and jet black in color. It framed her intelligent face and when disheveled, as it was now, gave several of the young men watching reason to pause and wonder about other ways it might become disheveled.

Greg Bolin watched the scene unfold from his third floor window, and smiled. This young lady must certainly be his new assistant. Very few visitors were allowed through the gate, and she matched the description he had been given. The company president, Joseph Philip Wooten - or Mr. J to most people - had told him that she was both beautiful and smart. The former was certainly true. Time would tell about the latter. Graduating Summa Cum Laude was a wonderful accomplishment and testified to her ability to regurgitate what she had read and heard, but could she think for herself? Somehow, looking at her now as she walked confidently towards the building entrance, Greg felt there probably wasn't much this new employee could not do, once challenged. He had no way of knowing that his life would end before he could appreciate the accuracy of this first impression.

Debra was from the small town of Sylvester, Georgia, less than two hundred miles from Condor's Atlanta headquarters. Two hundred miles and probably one hundred years, she had thought many times since her arrival in "Hotlanta," as the city was called in rural South Georgia. Growing up as the only child of Police Chief Patrick Raines and Barbara Raines, mother, schoolteacher, friend and confidant, she had heard many tales of the pitfalls of Atlanta.

Her father had lived here for twenty years working as an FBI agent, before moving to Sylvester with his wife and ten year old daughter to become that town's police chief. The job did not pay as well, but the cost of living was much less and with his income supplemented by the small FBI pension and with Barbara's salary as a schoolteacher, the Raines had lived quite nicely. Her father was well respected and, most importantly, according to both parents, he was home every night instead of on some dangerous assignment as when he was with the FBI. Debra always suspected her father missed the excitement of his former job, but if that were the case, he hid it well, seeming perfectly content with handling the minor crimes in the sleepy town that was now their home.

Barbara Raines had been an exemplary mother. Her job teaching high school biology enabled her to have the same schedule as her daughter. Debra had shown a rare aptitude for science as a small child, and her parents had encouraged her with her own laboratory. When her father jokingly complained that she was going to blow the house up (or worse) with some of her experiments, her mother only smiled. Mother and daughter spent many hours together in the small laboratory. It was easy for mother to become her confidant when they were working together. Debra could share her deepest thoughts and emotions, first date jitters, first crush, first heartbreak.

Debra was in her third year at Tennessee State, on a full scholastic scholarship, when her mother was killed in a freak accident on I-75, just 30 miles from home. She had called home at 5pm, as was her habit, to talk about her day. She felt a sense of dread when she was unable to reach anyone after hours of calling. Where could her parents go in Sylvester? When she heard her father's pained voice at 11p.m., she knew, even before his words confirmed her fear.

Somehow she had managed to get through that last year, then two years of graduate school. Classes, homework and exams were where she could excel and remember her mother's soft words of encouragement in that little home laboratory. Sports were her outlet for pent up emotional energy. Her social life became almost non-existent. Her boyfriend, Kent, had been by her side and tried to comfort her in the weeks immediately following her mother's death. But Debra had brushed him off so many times that he had drifted away - right into the arms of Mia Munson, beautiful, redheaded, statuesque, rival, and now local TV personality in Atlanta. Debra didn't really miss Kent. She had finally realized she just hated that he had taken up with Mia so readily. Far worse was her relationship with her father. The death of Barbara Raines left a void in both their lives, and father and daughter drifted apart, because seeing each other produced painful memories. They talked last night, though, and Debra smiled now as she recalled their conversation. It was like old times, with him telling her, "Be careful; keep your doors locked, and don't get taken in by the excitement of Atlanta." With this thought, Debra locked her new car, wondering again, "Why lock a convertible?" She walked into the reception area of Condor Pharmaceuticals Inc., for the first time.

♦♦♦

Greg Bolin turned from the window and sat back down at his desk. He forced himself to concentrate on the problem at hand. Getting a new assistant was fine, but it was another assistant, his chief researcher in fact, who was causing him problems now. Gene Windom knew. He could ruin them all if he wanted to. It appeared all he wanted was money, and if things went well, they could give him that. But once the faucet was opened, would it ever stop running?

He knew the others blamed him. They felt he should have known Windom would figure it out. But would that have really changed anything? He guessed that given what they knew now, they should have brought Windom in from the beginning. At least then he would be in the same boat as the other four and not in the position of being able to blackmail them and still be innocent of everything else. It was easy for them to look back at it now and know this, but at the time they were all thinking about the actual deed. None thought about Windom, and they all knew he was the chief researcher. Just because he happened to be under his supervision did not change that fact in Greg's mind. In any event it was way too late to turn back the clock.

They might be able to get him to sign the same agreement they all signed, in return for just being brought into the deal. If he agreed to do that, they would all be in the same boat, and he could not keep coming back to the trough. But, there was no incentive for him to do that, and Greg knew it. Mr. Wooten knew it too, and that really bothered Greg. Wooten was smooth, but he was not the type of man any person in his right mind would cross. He was not a person who would take being backed into a corner lightly. And he was going to be looking to Greg for some answers about how to deal with this problem.

Greg did not know it yet, but Wooten was way ahead of him. He had known what Greg's and the other's solution would be, and had discarded the idea as worthless. He had solved the problem, permanently. And he had solved it in a way that would affect them all. Starting today.

-7-

The busy receptionist gave Debra a smile, motioned her to one of several large comfortable chairs, and mouthed, "I'll be right with you," even as she answered the switchboard and transferred the third call since Debra had come inside.

Rather than sitting, Debra took the opportunity to look around at the many pictures of her new employer with powerful leaders. Even the President of the United States, it seemed, was a friend of Mr. Wooten. Dozens of plaques of appreciation, framed newspaper and magazine articles and the pictures took up almost an entire twenty-foot wall. Debra smiled again at her good fortune. She smoothed her plaid skirt and looked in the mirror behind the chairs. Her hair, so recently tousled, now fell into curls that framed her face perfectly. Once the source of teasing and angst, her naturally curly hair was now a godsend, requiring little maintenance. She wore very little makeup, just a little mascara to highlight her hazel eyes and lipstick.

As she wondered for at least the hundredth time if she were dressed properly for this first day at work, she heard the receptionist call, "You must be Ms. Raines. We have been expecting you."

"Please, call me Debra," she said, as she turned to the young lady of about eighteen, who was smiling at her.

The badge claimed she was Beth Simmons and the girl confirmed that by saying, "And I'm Beth. Here, put on this visitor's badge so security won't boot you out!" She handed Debra a badge marked "visitor" with her name typed neatly on the surface.

"I will tell Mr. J you are on the way up. His office is on the twentieth floor, and the elevator is just over there."

Beth motioned towards the bank of windows to her left, and Debra saw for the first time the stainless steel doors of six modern elevators, shined to a mirror finish by the custodian, who even now was cleaning some perceived speck of dust from one of the doors.

"Jim will take you up," Beth said as a security officer appeared from nowhere.

Jim Billups, the badge proclaimed, and Debra smiled into the kind eyes of the officer who was about her age, with closely cropped hair and a neatly laundered uniform that did little to conceal the muscular physique of someone who spent many hours in the gym.

They shook hands as he said, "Nice to meet you, Ms. Raines, welcome to Condor."

He led her to the elevators, and they entered. The officer passed a card by a sensing device and one of the doors opened immediately. He pressed the button for the top floor. As the door shut their images were reflected perfectly in the polished aluminum. Debra was pleased to see the anxiety she felt about her first day at work was not reflected in her countenance. She could tell the security guard was also studying her, while trying not to be seen doing so.

She smiled at him and said, "Have you worked here long?" Her voice was confidant and friendly.

"About three years. It is a good company. They pay us well, and we have good benefits. I am sure you will like it here - everyone does," he smiled.

Debra smiled back and knew the guard's welcome was sincere. They talked about the weather for the next few seconds, and then the door opened.

"Here you are," said Officer Billups, "I will leave you here. It was nice talking to you."

Debra smiled and said thank you, as she exited the elevator, and the door closed. Turning, Debra was greeted by yet another receptionist.

"Hello, Ms. Raines. I am Donna Mims, Mr. Wooten's secretary."

Debra shook the offered hand and smiled at the middle aged, attractive woman.

"Hello. Please call me Debra. I am pleased to meet you."

"Come right this way. Mr. Wooten is waiting for you."

The secretary smiled. Debra noted that she called her boss by his sir name, no first names, or nicknames, and that she did not offer her first name, either. She followed the professional looking woman into an enormous office with plush carpeting and beautiful wood paneled walls. Mr. Wooten and two other gentlemen stood as she entered, and Debra knew they were discussing her as their conversation stopped in mid-stream. She felt the appraising eyes of the other men as she accepted Mr. Wooten's outstretched hand. Her eyes quickly took in the bank of televisions behind her new boss, all turned to 24-hour news and stock channels. The gun cabinet to the side of his enormous desk was filled with rifles, and there were more pictures of her boss, but this time the pictures featured slain animals of all sorts. Bear, deer, elk, fox and even a lion stared back at her. Evidently, Mr. Wooten enjoyed hunting of all types.

"Good, morning Debra! Welcome to Condor Pharmaceuticals! I was just telling these fellows how fortunate we are to have you on board. Meet Tim Murray, our Vice President of Personnel, and Bill Horton, our financial and accounting V.P."

Debra smiled and replied "Good morning! It is very nice to meet you, and I feel like I am the one who is fortunate. Everything I read and hear about this company is so good! I am very excited to be here".

Mr. Wooten, motioned with his perfectly manicured hand, and all took their seats.

"I asked these fellows to be here so they can give you a little more insight into our company, and exactly what you will be doing," he said. "Why don't you go first, Tim"?

Tim Murray cleared his throat and smiled at Debra as she turned slightly to face him. He was a pleasant looking man of about forty-five, Debra judged. His hair was thick and neatly combed and had just the slightest hint of gray at his temples. He was impeccably dressed, wearing a striped shirt and matching tie that accentuated his rail thin frame. His smile revealed perfect teeth, white and straight and Debra knew they must be capped. Just too perfect.

"Condor is a relatively small company, as pharmaceutical companies go. We have just fewer than three hundred people on our payroll. However, we believe that we have the cream of the crop, especially when it comes to our research group, which makes up about a third of our staff. We also have a higher profit margin than the "big boys," partly because of a lower overhead, and partly because we have a very stable market for our products. We have a number of drugs such as LOPRO, which is our blood pressure lowering medication, and several more that are about ready for FDA approval. The most exciting of these is CHOLOW, which is destined to become the leading cholesterol lowering medicine. We are hoping for approval within weeks. We believe it is so far superior to other staten medications that it will virtually capture that entire market. In addition, we have a subsidiary company, CONTACT, Inc., which produces a number of medical and personal hygiene products, such as surgical masks, and 'Antibaids', which are band-aids with antibiotic medicine already applied to the pad. A relatively new product is the Oxi-pure device, which is a personal air purifier that can be powered by batteries and worn around an individual's neck. We think it will have a great reception among people with allergies and other respiratory problems, as well as in hospitals where it can reduce to almost nothing the risk of getting airborne infections.

You will be working with Dr. Greg Bolin, who heads up our research department. You will find Dr. Bolin fair, but demanding, to work for. He is an absolute genius when it comes to isolating the genes that cause diseases and developing vaccines for them. There are about seventy people working in that department, not counting the support staff, such as secretaries, security, and custodial.

Security is a big deal at Condor. You would not have gotten through the gate this morning if Mr. Wooten had not provided the officers with your photo and had you pre-approved for admittance. When we finish here, we will take you down to meet the head of security so you can go through orientation and get your permanent ID badge and retina check."

As the vice president finished, Debra said, "Wow. I knew about Condor and its great reputation. But I did not know about CONTACT. I have heard of a retina scan, but how exactly does it work?"

"The process is simple and painless. We actually do it in-house at the same time you get your security card, and it only takes a few seconds. The card will let you enter the building and use the elevators, open doors to the cafeteria and such, but to enter the laboratories where you will be working, you will first have to look into a device that scans your retina. The retina is much like a fingerprint, in that everyone's is unique. However, unlike a fingerprint, it cannot be replicated."

Debra started to ask more questions about that, but decided that was probably for another time and place, ...and person.

Mr. Wooten said, "We have to be very careful about security around here. We spend many millions on research and cannot afford any leaks. Fortunately, your security clearance came back perfect," he smiled. "Thanks, Tim. Now it is your turn, Bill."

Bill Horton could not have been more different in appearance than Tim Murray. Where Tim was tall and thin, Bill was short and stocky. His suit, while clean and neat, was too tight and did not complement him. He wore glasses that slightly magnified his intelligent brown eyes. He took out a handkerchief, wiped his brow, and began.

"Condor is very solid company with sales exceeding 600 million dollars. This includes sales from CONTACT, which is a wholly owned subsidiary. We spend several hundred million each year on research alone. And Tim is right; we have some very good products, and a loyal following."

Debra watched the financial officer carefully as he droned on about figures and percentages. There was something that she could not put her finger on that did not seem right. She was very big on eye contact, and Horton never held the contact. Instead he would glance at her and look nervously away. She did not imagine that a new hire would make the Vice President of Finance nervous, but something certainly was. She noticed he glanced toward Mr. Wooten often, and Debra wondered if that was the source of the man's problem. She told herself to forget it - it was probably her imagination anyway.

"And so you have indeed chosen a very stable company to work with," Horton finished.

Debra smiled appreciatively and wondered if she had missed anything of great import.

"Well Debra, I hope you feel as good about coming to work here as we do about having you here," Mr. Wooten said. "I am sorry to rush you, but I have another meeting shortly," he said, standing. "I will be talking to you more in the near future. Tim, would you please escort her down to security, and then show her around and take her to the lab? Bill, please stay. I have a couple of things for you."

Debra shook hands with the president and with Bill Horton as they said their goodbyes.

-8-

Mia Munson smiled at the camera and said, "That's it for tonight. Please join us again tomorrow, and we will update you on all the latest. Remember. You will hear it first on NewsNow, Channel 4, WXYA." The camera pulled back, and Mia and her two associates sat, smiles frozen, until the red light on the camera went out.

"It is HOT," Mia said standing. I thought my make up would start running any minute. We have got to get that AC running again!"

"You've got that right! I think I'm stuck to the chair!" said Toni Terrell, the other female of the news trio, and the weather forecaster.

"Yeah, well at least you don't have to wear a jacket and tie," said Brian Marcot, the third member, standing, revealing jeans beneath his suit jacket. "I'm going to check with James and find out what the problem is," he said, referring to the news director/operating officer/boss of the show.

"Please tell him we just can't do another segment with it this hot," said Mia. "I'll see ya'll tomorrow. I've got to run. Kent is taking me to a late dinner. I've got to shower and change. See ya'll tomorrow!"

Toni and Brian smiled at each other. "I'm glad I'm married. It is hard enough to do this job without having to juggle dating and all," said Toni.

"Yeah, me too," said Brian. "I'm going to see James. See you tomorrow."

Mia Munson was as striking off camera as she was on. She was a little thinner than she appeared on TV, but she managed it without looking emaciated the way some TV personalities did. Her naturally red, straight hair that she wore shoulder length, glowed with vitality. She had a small ridge of freckles around her perfect nose, which were not visible under the heavy make up she wore on-camera. In person, the freckles did nothing to take away from her beauty. In fact, they gave her face extra character and made her even more appealing. She had worked her way up to anchor of the local news show over the last three years.

Kent was her long-time boyfriend and confidant. They began dating when she was a senior in college. Mia had assumed for some time they would get married one day, but Kent seemed perfectly content with things as they were. He had never mentioned marriage, but Mia knew he had no other girl friends. She wasn't quite sure how she was going to move this relationship to the next stage, but she felt compelled to do so. She still aimed for more successes as a news anchor, but she was very aware that she was not getting any younger. She wanted the security of marriage, and she wanted to start a family someday. Kent Bridges would be her husband sooner rather than later Mia determined, as she washed the TV make-up from her face and brushed her hair. She quickly changed blouses and surveyed herself in the full-length mirror. Smiling at herself, she turned and walked outside to meet her future husband.

-9-

The insistent ring of the phone awakened Jack Nebra at five in the morning. He was instantly alert - heart pounding, as he grabbed the phone. Good news never came this early. If the phone rings between midnight and six o'clock, it has to be bad news. Despite his many years in law enforcement, he just never had been able to get past the heart pounding adrenalin rush that came every time he was awakened like this.

"Nebra,"he exclaimed into the phone.

"Jack, we've had a home invasion and killing. Here's the address."

Jack jotted down the address. "Any witnesses?" he asked. He listened for a minute and asked a few more questions. "I'll be there in thirty. Tell them to hang loose." He had crossed the apartment and turned on the coffee pot, then returned to the bathroom and turned on the shower as he talked. Hanging up the phone, he brushed his teeth, used the toilet and jumped into the shower. Fifteen minutes later he was in the car with a hot cup of coffee and a cinnamon breakfast bar.

Jack turned into the well-kept neighborhood and was guided to the scene by the flashing lights of the two patrol cars that were parked out front. He parked his black, unmarked police car in front of the house and walked up the driveway. He had to duck under the familiar yellow crime scene tape about half way up the drive. He was greeted by a couple of officers and was told that sergeant Gaily was inside the house. Nebra smiled. He liked Gaily and knew the man, a veteran officer with over twenty years of service, would have protected the crime scene for him. Jack entered the house and followed his ears to the master bedroom.

Gene Windom was lying on his back between the bed and the bathroom door. A forty five-caliber pistol was inches away from his right hand. Death was never a pretty sight. Blood surrounded the man and had turned brown as it dried in the carpet. Photographers were taking pictures of the corpse and the room. Gaily looked up and smiled grimly at the detective.

"Hey, Jack, looks like we have another sorry mess to deal with."

Jack shook hands with the Sergeant and asked, "What have we got so far?"

"Well, the house is registered to a Gene Windom, and I assume that's who this is, although we do not have a positive ID yet. We received the call from the alarm service about two-thirty. One of the neighbors came over after we arrived. The house alarm siren was blasting away and had wakened him. We found the panel in the hall closet and disconnected it. It was the loudest siren I've ever heard. Anyway, the neighbor said Windom lived alone, was divorced and had two young daughters who came every other weekend. He had not heard any gunshots, but he did see a car going past his house after the siren went off. Since this is a cul-de-sac, the car must have come from here. He didn't recognize the car, and it was too far away for him to even be able to tell what kind it was. We did not get him to identify the body cause we really didn't know what we had yet. We found the guy's billfold on the bathroom counter. His driver's license picture sure looks like him.

We will get hold of his ex for the formal ID....I'll let you, the hot-shot detective, figure out everything that happened, but it looks like someone broke in and the deceased got out of bed, hit the panic button over there," he pointed at the button on the wall, "and got his gun. The killer got him first and probably panicked at the noise before he could search the place, 'cause it doesn't appear to be ransacked, and the guy's wallet was just laying on the bathroom sink, with sixty bucks in it and credit cards."

Nebra stepped over the body and entered the bathroom. It was clean, at least cleaner than his. There was a walk-in closet with door open and he could see that all the clothes were lined up neatly; pants on the bottom hangers, shirts on the top. Long sleeves together and short selves together. The guy had been neat, or he had a good housekeeper. He walked back through the house and noticed the sit-and-spin in the family room. More children without a father. What a waste. There was a plate and salad bowl in the sink, rinsed of course. He did not see a glass, but then found it sitting on the bar counter top, along with half a bottle of good Scotch. There was a pair of shoes beside the recliner. Evidently the guy had eaten supper, had a few drinks and sat in the recliner, probably watching a movie. The detective wondered, as he often did in these situations, what the guy would have done differently had he known this was his last night alive. His bet was that very few people would have acted exactly as they did if they knew in advance of their death.

The detective picked up a tablet of paper off the coffee table. Evidently, the deceased was a doodler. "Balium =s Sars Conference =s Hong Kong." Probably nothing. But he did call a cameraman to take a picture of the tablet he laid back on the table. He then put the paper in an evidence bag. He walked back to the front door and examined the lock. He was unable to detect any obvious signs of tampering. There were a few scratches, but they could have come from normal use. He examined the door casing and found a sticky residue from the duct tape. He had the cameraperson take pictures of that and made another note in his notebook.

The coroner had arrived and made his cursory examination. With Jack's approval, they loaded the deceased on a gurney for transportation to the morgue.

"We'll get in touch with the next of kin for the formal ID," Jack said. "How long before you do the autopsy."

"We'll be done around two this afternoon. If you can't get someone to ID before 10, just wait 'til after two."

Nebra nodded his head. "Deal. I'll let you know as soon as we get in touch with someone."

Jack walked the coroner to the door and saw two TV news trucks at the street, cameras panning back and forth between the house and their respective news reporters. They were both female, both young. "Vultures," he thought.

He turned back to the bedroom. Now that the body was gone, it was time to get as much information about the man as possible. He started with the billfold. Taking everything out and laying it neatly on the sink top, he had it photographed before examining the contents. The drivers' license showed the man was forty years old, barely. The insurance card was with Blue Cross and showed the employer to be The Condor Corporation. There were two pictures of young girls about five and seven, both pretty and innocent looking. And now fatherless, he thought. There were a few credit cards and receipts, but nothing else of value to him. He started opening drawers and looking for information.

An assistant detective, Joel Smith, joined him. Nebra brought him up to speed, and they continued the slow process of finding out all they could about the man who had formerly occupied this dwelling. From the kitchen Smith retrieved the Rolodex that had the man's important phone numbers in it. Another officer was dusting for fingerprints. About nine a.m., an officer at the street used the radio to call Nebra. There was a lady down there who was almost hysterical. She had been watching television and seen the news reports and recognized the subdivision name and the pictures of her ex-husband's house. She wanted to talk to someone who could tell her what was going on.

"Notification by television," Nebra thought. "Welcome to America." He assigned Smith the job of talking to the lady and taking her to the morgue for the formal identification. He was going to the Condor Corporation.

♦♦♦

Rex Slaton had slept fitfully. Even though he had gotten to bed well after three, he was up at seven-thirty. He felt better after a shower and a cup of coffee. He missed seeing his son, who was out the door for school by the time he was up. He had a bowl of cereal with his coffee, grabbed an apple for later and kissed his wife good-bye. He knew his boss would want to hear from him ASAP.

Slaton entered the Condor building and was just hanging up his coat, when he got a call from the main gate that a detective was there, wanting admittance. Apparently, an employee of the company had been killed, and the detective wanted to talk to personnel. Slaton instructed the gate guard to let Nebra in and to tell him he would meet the man at the receptionist's desk in the lobby.

"Damn, that was quick," he thought.

His office was on the first floor, just a few steps away from the front desk, so he was waiting on the detective when he came into the building. He introduced himself to Nebra, and they exchanged business cards. He walked him back to his office.

"Please excuse the mess, I have been swamped the last few days. Have a seat and tell me what this is about. Would you like coffee?"

Nebra sat in one of two chairs in front of Slaton's desk and gratefully accepted the offer of coffee. "Last night a man was killed in a home invasion. We won't have a formal ID for a little while, but we believe the man to be Gene Windom. The insurance card in his wallet says he is employed here. If he was, I would like to see his personnel file."

"Oh no! Gene's worked here for years. That's terrible! Whatever I can do to help, I will. Normally that information is confidential, but under the circumstances, I'll be glad to provide you with whatever you need. If you want to look at the actual file, it will take a few minutes to get it from personnel. But if you want to see it on the computer, I can pull it up right here," Slaton said.

"I think I'd better look at the actual file, if you don't mind."

"No problem," Slaton said, as he lifted the phone.

"Someone will bring it down in just a few minutes," Slaton said. "You say this was a home invasion? Was anyone else hurt?"

"No, it appears the guy lived alone. A neighbor said he was divorced. He had two small kids."

"That's too bad. I used to be a cop, and I've seen my share of that kind of thing. It's never any fun."

"Yeah, that's right. Where were you a cop?"

The men continued to make small talk for about ten minutes. Nebra, ever the detective, soon knew just about all there was to know about Slaton's police career, or at least all that Slaton would tell. Jim Billups knocked on Slaton's door, entered and gave the security chief a thin file folder. Slaton opened it and commented, "Not much here," as he gave it to the detective.

Nebra took out his notepad and copied down Windom's now ex-wife's name and the names of his children. He noted that his father was deceased, but his mother lived in Rochester, N.Y. There was information obtained while getting the security clearance for Windom, copies of his college transcripts and very little else. It showed he worked in the development and research section of Condor.

It was this last item that Nebra asked about. "What exactly does the research section do?"

"Well, they research and try to develop drugs to cure or help various diseases and sicknesses such as cancer, high blood pressure and arthritis. They take up several floors of the building. It is quite impressive. I don't know exactly what Mr. Windom worked on. You would have to ask the section head about that."

"And who would that be?"

"Greg Bolin heads up that section. I'll get him to come down, if you like."

"Yes, I think I probably need to talk to him, see if he knows why anyone would want Windom dead."

Slaton looked at Nebra, puzzled. "You mean you think this was something other than a robbery gone bad?"

"No, not at all. I'm just trying to cover all the bases. I have no reason to think it was anything other than that, but I have a dead man, and I owe it to him to try and find his killer. So I look at everything and hope something leads me in the right direction. You know how it is."

"Yeah, I know," said Slaton, relieved, as he picked up the phone to call Greg Bolin.

They were interrupted by Slaton's intercom. "Mr. Slaton, sorry to interrupt, but Mr. Murray and a Ms. Raines are here to see you."

Slaton paused and put the phone down. "Mr. Murray is our Vice President of Personnel. He needs to know about this."

Nebra nodded and shrugged his shoulders.

Slaton pushed his intercom button and said, "Please ask Mr. Murray to come in, and get Ms. Raines something to drink while she waits."

There was a quick knock on the door, and Tim Murray stuck his head in. "Sorry, Rex, I didn't know you had someone with you."

"Come in, Mr. Murray. This matter will need your attention, too, I'm afraid." Murray came in and Slaton and Nebra stood as introductions were made.

"I'm afraid that we have had a tragedy." Slaton said, as Nebra and Murray shook hands. "Gene Windom, who works with Greg Bolin's outfit, was killed last night in a home invasion. Detective Nebra is handling the investigation. He has looked over Mr. Windom's personnel file and I was just getting ready to call Mr. Bolin, so he could talk to him."

Murray quickly sat down, and his face turned white. "Oh, my God. Are you sure?"

Nebra said, "We don't have the official ID yet, but yeah I'm sure." Just then, Nebra's cell phone rang, and he answered it and listened for a moment. "Okay, thanks. I'm at Condor now.

I'll call you back later." He hung up and looked at the two men. "It's official now. His ex-wife has confirmed the deceased is Windom."

Tim Murray covered his face with his right hand. "Oh, my God," he said again. "I just can't believe this."

Nebra noted that Murray's hand was shaking, and his face was pasty white. He chalked it up as just a lot of concern for a co-worker. Plus, anytime there is an untimely death, especially if it's murder, people are always horrified.

"Yeah, I know," he said. "It's tough. He had two young children. It's good they were not staying with him last night. Now we need to try and find out who did it."

Murray collected himself and asked, "What can we do?"

"Well nothing, probably. I just need to talk to his supervisor, Mr."...he glanced at his notes, "Bolin."

Murray looked at Slaton. "Why don't we get Detective Nebra a badge, and I'll take him up to the third floor conference room. Call Bolin and get him to meet us there. That way you can take care of Ms. Raines. She is the new hire and she's waiting outside. She'll be working for Bolin, too."

"Okay, sounds good." He picked up the phone and called Greg Bolin. It took a minute for his secretary to get him. When he came on the line, Slaton explained the situation to him. Nebra, who had heard Bolin answer the phone, heard absolutely no comment.

"Mr. Bolin, Mr. Murray is here, and he is bringing the detective up to the third floor conference room. Can you meet them there?"

Nebra heard Bolin say yes, and Slaton hung up the phone.

The men all stood and Slaton said, "It was a pleasure meeting you, detective. I'm sorry it had to be like this, though."

Nebra shook his hand and said "Thanks. I may need to call you back. I guess this is the best way to reach you?" he asked, looking at the business card Slaton had given to him.

"That's it. I'll be glad to help any way I can. Don't hesitate to call."

"Thanks, talk to you later." He followed Tim Murray out of the security chief's office.

Debra Raines was seated on a love seat in the outer office, leafing through a magazine.

Murray said, "Sorry to keep you, Ms. Raines. Something has come up that I need to tend to, but Mr. Slaton here is our Chief of Security, and he'll take care of you. Rex, this is Ms. Raines."

Slaton and Debra shook hands as Nebra watched from the side. Very, very nice, he thought to himself. Debra and Nebra smiled and nodded at each other briefly.

Without bothering to introduce them Murray said, "Let's go this way, detective, and we'll get you a visitors badge."

The two men walked off and Debra and Slaton went back into his office.

-10-

After Debra and Tim Murray left, Jim Wooten turned to Bill Horton. "I hope Bolin has better luck with her than he had with Windom. I know we meet on this tomorrow, but have you been thinking about it?"

"I've thought of little else, boss, but I don't have any more ideas except to bring him into the group and buy his silence."

Wooten looked at his V.P. tiredly. "Well, okay then. We'll meet tomorrow."

Horton, dismissed, said, "Yes sir. I'll be here," and left the office.

Wooten glanced at the clock. He had not slept well last night, wondering about Windom and Slaton. He knew that Murray was on the way to Slaton's office now with Debra. He picked up the phone and dialed the security office. Slaton's secretary answered.

"Is he in? This is Jim Wooten."

"Yes sir, he is here. He has some detective in with him now. Do you want me to interrupt?"

Wooten was stunned. A detective! "No," he said quickly. "Just ask him to call when he gets an opportunity."

He hung up the phone and sat, thinking. Wooten had known he was taking a risk. How could a detective be here already? He didn't scare easily, but at this moment Jim Wooten felt very vulnerable, and yes, a little scared. He turned to the bank of televisions and turned the volume up on one. It was the good-looking redhead from Channel Four NewsNow.

"We are following the story that broke early this morning about a home invasion and killing in Douglas County," said Mia Munson. "We go live to the scene now with our traveling reporter, Van Carter. What's new Van?"

"Well Mia, what we know for sure is there was a home invasion in this upscale neighborhood last night that left a man dead. The police aren't giving out his name, of course, until next of kin are notified. They did tell us a short while ago there was no one else in the house. The neighbors here are pretty shaken up."

The camera panned, showing the house in the back of a wooded lot and coming back to Carter who was now standing with one of the neighbors.

"This is Greg Fordham, who lives next door. Tell us what happened, Mr. Fordham."

"Well, about two o'clock I was awakened by the siren from the house here. I got up and turned on the lights and saw a car driving off. But it was too far away to see anything. I called 911, and they said the police had been dispatched. That's all I know. I just can't believe that something like this happened in my neighborhood. We have never had any trouble in here. It's just frightening."

"There you have it, Mia. Back to you."

Mia Munson gave a sincere half-smile. "Stay tuned to Channel Four, NewsNow. We'll be following this breaking story all morning and will bring you the latest information on this sad situation, as it comes to us."

Wooten sat back in his chair and turned the volume back down. So, it had happened. And now there was a detective in Slaton's office. What did that mean? Surely Slaton had not left something there to tie him to the murder. He was smarter than that, wasn't he? Wooten was not a very happy man.

Slaton's secretary handed him the message to call Mr. Wooten. He looked at it and turned back to Debra Raines. "Ms. Raines, would you mind waiting out here for just a minute? I need to make a quick phone call."

"Sure," said Debra, "no problem. I'll be right here." She smiled and sat down on the loveseat.

Slaton went into his office and called Wooten. Wooten quickly answered the phone when his secretary announced the call.

"What is happening?"

"Well, things didn't go according to plan, and our friend had an accident. The detective found his health insurance card that showed he worked here. It's just a routine follow-up. He..."

"Stop," said Wooten, interrupting. "Come up here. We'll talk about it when you get here."

"Sir, I've got Ms. Raines outside in the hall. I can go over things with her quickly and then get officer Billups to take her for her retina scan and ID card and the rest."

Wooten thought for a minute. He was reassured by the 'routine part.' "Okay, do that, but make it quick."

He hung up and sat back, still nervous, and still frightened. It was one thing to contemplate a crime like murder; quite another to actually carry it out. Especially when you might get caught.

♦♦♦

Nebra and Murray exited the elevator on the third floor and turned right. The conference room was the first door on the right. It had taken them a few minutes to get the visitor's pass and Greg Bolin was waiting for them. Murray made the introductions and a very nervous Bolin shook hands with the detective. Nebra was used to people being nervous when questioned about a homicide, but Bolin's condition was excessive.

The men sat down and Bolin asked, "What's happened?"

Nebra gave him the Reader's Digest version of the night's events and asked "What can you tell me about Mr. Windom? Did he have any enemies that you know of? Was he a gambler? What kind of employee was he?"

Bolin, still nervous, answered, "Well, he was a really great employee. He was my top research assistant. He had been with the company about fifteen years. I don't really think he had any enemies. I know he was divorced, but he and his ex-wife seemed to get along okay. He was devoted to his two girls and would sometimes leave early to go to events they were involved in at school. He dated some, but I don't think he had a steady girlfriend. I really don't know much more than that."

"What was he working on?"

" Well, he actually was working on a couple of projects. We have been trying to find a cure for the common cold, just like everybody else. That was his specialty project. The other one was an arthritis medicine."

"When did you see him last?"

"Yesterday morning." He had come in early and gotten some work done. Then he had taken the rest of the day off."

"Did he say why?"

Bolin had beads of perspiration on his brow, even though the room was quite comfortable, maybe even a little chilly.

"Well, no, he didn't. Actually, we had a few words about the project and ... and, well, I told him to take the day off and think about it."

"Words? Do you mean an argument?"

"No, no. He was just upset at how long it took to get things approved by the FDA. He was just frustrated, and I didn't think he could be productive in his frame of mind, so I told him to take the day off."

Nebra regarded the man a moment. That might explain the man's nervousness. He had words with an employee and sent him home. Then the guy gets killed and a homicide detective is here questioning him. He decided to reassure the man.

"Look, Mr. Bolin, I'm just trying to get information about Mr. Windom. Someone killed him, and I want to find that person. He worked for you, so naturally I need to question you. But you are not a suspect. We don't have any suspects yet. This is probably a random home invasion that went bad. A nice house in a nice neighborhood means money. So just relax and try to help me out."

Bolin wiped his brow and replied a little more calmly. "Okay, I'll do what I can. I just don't know that much about his personal life."

Nebra glanced over at Murray, who had stayed in the room. "Did you know Windom? Is there anything you can tell me about him?"

"Well, as Greg said, he had been with us for a good long time. He was highly regarded and he seemed to get along well with the other employees. We did not socialize together, but I have seen him out on occasion. You know, like at a restaurant. He always had a date, but I don't think I ever saw him with the same girl."

Nebra consulted his notes. He turned back to Greg Bolin. "Does the word "Balium" mean anything to you?

-II-

ebra Raines was feeling a little confused. She knew
something was wrong, but not what. The initial
meeting with Mr. Wooten and the others had gone well. But
now, she felt like she was being passed around like a basketball.
First, Mr. Murray had passed her off to Slaton, with barely an
introduction before he rushed off with the good-looking guy
they had not even bothered to introduce her to. Now Slaton
was passing her off to Officer Billups after a very hurried and
general introduction to security measures at Condor. And now,
he was rushing off somewhere. At least Officer Billups seemed
to not be hurried. He was very friendly and informative,
explaining all about the retina scan, how the security cards
worked, the layout of the building and so forth.

"This is the cafeteria," he now said, as he led her into a small
but well appointed dining area. "Some of us like to bring our
lunch at least part of the time instead of always going out. In
addition to the tables out here, there are a couple of
microwaves, a small grill and two refrigerators in the back.

There are two 30 cup coffee pots, one for decaf and one for regular. The custodian keeps a pretty good watch over them so you can always get a hot cup of coffee. Of course, there are also the small break rooms on every other floor, and there is coffee in those, too. This is the only one that has the snack machines and soft drink machines though."

Jim Billups completed the tour of the building with the pretty new-hire. She seemed very nice and friendly, and he was impressed with her charm and good looks. All in all, this had been a very pleasurable day for him. But, now it was time to walk her to the research lab and for him to get back to his normal duties.

They exited at the third floor, and Billups took her past the empty conference room and through the swinging doors leading into the research area.

"Why don't you go ahead and use your new card and the retina scan so we can be sure everything is working properly."

Debra inserted her card into the small machine with the blinking red light at the left of the door. There was an audible click and the light turned green. Billups opened the door, and they entered the next room. The retina scan machine was the only item in the room. The door leading into the research area was not even equipped with a doorknob. Debra walked over to the machine, rested her chin in the cup and looked into the small camera-type lens. There was another audible click, and the door to the research lab opened on its own. They entered the research area, and Debra looked around.

"So this is where I'll earn my keep," she mused to herself.

Debra was not sure exactly what she had expected, but she was not surprised at what she saw. There was a long hallway leading in both directions from the entrance door. On either side of the corridor were several large rooms with big glass windows opening to the corridor. As they walked, she could see people in lab coats working with microscopes and computers. In another room she saw cages with mice and a few monkeys. In another there were just cubicles with people working diligently. As they went further down the corridor, they started passing private offices.

Officer Billups spoke, "We could have gone around the other way and reached the private offices first, but I thought you might like to see this area first."

"Oh, thanks, I did. This looks really exciting. Just think, right here someone could find the cure for cancer or something."

"Yeah, I think about that too, every time I come by here. Well, here we are," he said as they entered a large office with a reception area.

They walked up to the secretary's desk, and Officer Billups introduced her.

"Hello, Jane. This is Ms. Raines. I believe ya'll have been expecting her. Ms. Raines, This is Ms. Hightower."

The two women shook hands, and each gave the other their first name.

"We finally finished up the tour, and she has been through security orientation and has her card and retina scan, so I'll go on. Ms. Raines, I enjoyed showing you around. Ya'll have a good day." Officer Billups gave them a mock salute, as he left them alone.

Jane Hightower was in her early fifties, almost as tall as Debra, and was very trim. She wore a simple white blouse, a navy skirt and sensible shoes without heels. She smiled warmly at Debra, and Debra liked her instantly.

"Mr. Bolin had to go to an important meeting with Mr. Wooten. It is already past lunchtime. If you don't have other plans, why don't you and I go out and get something to eat? Maybe, he'll be back when we are done."

"That would be great," Debra said. "I don't have any plans at all. In fact, since I'm new to this area, I wouldn't even know where to go, so that would be a big help."

"Just one minute," Jane said as she picked up the phone and told someone she was leaving for lunch, putting the phone on call forward.

The two women exited the building into the hot sunshine. "Do you want me to drive?" asked Debra, motioning towards the red Miata.

Jane looked at the car and smiled. "That car looks like fun, but I don't know if I can get in it. Besides, I know the way, so let's take mine. It's right here."

The two women got into a blue Crown Victoria that was about twice the size of the Miata.

"It's not as sporty as yours, but it has great air conditioning, and I'm an old woman who likes her comfort," Jane joked. For a second, Debra was reminded of her mother, and she liked Jane even more. The two women talked easily as Jane drove.

-12-

Mia Munson was changing into street clothes in the dressing room of NewsNow. She was tired, because she had worked the early evening news the night before, gone out to eat with Kent, and then had to be at work by five for the morning news. She did not often work the morning news, but Michelle, the morning news regular, was on vacation, and she was filling in. Michelle could return the favor in November, when Mia went on vacation. It had been pretty much a standard news day. An apartment fire that destroyed an eight unit building in Decatur, caused by some idiot who had decided to set his grill on top of the air conditioner. When the unit came on, it blew sparks into the attic. Now eight families had pretty much lost everything. Two teenagers killed and one injured while racing a BMW and losing control. The tree won. A mugging on MARTA, the local mass transit system that seemed to be forever in the news for mis-management or something. And the home invasion, and killing in Douglas County. Murder stories were always good for "live at the scene" reports. Four good local human-interest stories, she thought, as she left the building. On the national scene, the seemingly never-ending saga of the SARS epidemic was also in the news today. More and more people were sick and dying in China. Now, the sickness had shown up in Canada with two confirmed deaths. The CDC had issued a travel advisory against traveling to Canada, and that Government was beside itself. All in all, it was a pretty good day for news reporters.

Mia drove slowly home to her midtown cottage and thought about the night before. She just knew that Kent would propose any day now. But, he had not yet done so. Last night, they dined at a small, cozy restaurant in Buckhead. The food was good, the wine was wonderful, and it was an intimate occasion. It was the perfect time for him to propose. But he hadn't. Her feelings were in turmoil, and she knew that she was too tired now to try and sort them out.

She thought back to the time in college when she and Kent had started going out. They enjoyed a few classes together, but had not gone out. Kent was involved with a sorority sister of hers, Debra Raines. Debra's mom had been killed in an auto accident, and the girl had pretty much gone off the deep end. Kent had talked to her for hours about Debra after the accident. According to him, Debra just shut him out of her life. He had tried to be there for her, but she became obsessive with her schoolwork and sports and pretty much ignored Kent. Initially, Kent had confided in Mia, because he knew her and knew she and Debra were in the same sorority. Mia told him that Debra was probably just so emotionally hurt that she was afraid to be close to anyone at that time. Shortly after that, Kent had asked her out, and they had been dating exclusively for over three years.

Mia turned into the driveway of her yuppie midtown cottage. She had bought the two bedroom / one bath home a little over a year ago and immediately set about fixing it up herself. It was beautiful, she thought now. The exterior was a pale yellow with white trim and blue shutters. The huge front porch had two porch swings and several chairs and was a pleasant place to sit and people watch. But not now. She resolved to go straight to bed and sort her feelings out when she was clear-headed. But, she thought, it's time for Kent to propose or let me know why. She set her clock for four P.M. because she had to be back at the station by five. That will give me six hours sleep she thought. Not enough, but at least I don't have to pull another morning shift. She shut the heavy drapes and climbed into the four-poster bed. She turned out the lamp and was asleep instantly.

-13-

Patrick Raines, former FBI agent, current police chief and Debra Raines' father, was taking the afternoon off. He had not been fishing in a month of Sundays, and he intended to rectify that situation. A friend of his had a small private lake between Sylvester and Albany, and Patrick had a standing invitation to use the lake and the small fishing boat that was kept there. He loaded three rods and reels and a cooler with a couple of beers and soft drinks into his civilian vehicle, a late model Ford F-150 truck, and headed out. He made one stop, at Buster's Barbeque, for a couple of smoked pork sandwiches with outside meat. He had called ahead to make sure the small, to-go-only barbeque place was open. Buster had the best barbeque anywhere around, but he wasn't very dependable. He would smoke the meat, and then just sell it all and take a few days off. He kept no set business hours and never bothered collecting any sales tax. Chief Raines was quite sure that no taxes were ever paid, either. But like everyone else in this small town, he did not care. Everybody paid too many taxes anyway.

Besides, when he was there, Buster was extremely likable and colorful. And he made great barbeque.

It was only about a fifteen-minute drive to the lake, which was good, thought Chief Raines, 'cause the sandwiches were smelling good.' He drove right up to the lake bank and parked. He decided to feed himself before he fed the fish. He sat in his truck eating Bubba's Barbeque and drinking a Foster's beer, listening to the news. There was a little information about the travel advisory against traveling to Canada because of the SARS epidemic, and a little local news. There was nothing about Atlanta. His thoughts, however, were entirely on Atlanta, or rather on his daughter, who had just moved there.

Lunch finished, he boarded the small fishing boat and rowed towards a likely area where he could see a fallen tree partially rising above the water. He put a cricket on one rod and spinner bait on another. He hoped to catch some large bass on the spinner, and he was sure the cricket would attract plenty of bream, pronounced "brim" in these parts.

As he cast his line, his thoughts returned to his daughter. Theirs had always been a close family. But when his wife had been killed, they somehow drifted apart. He knew the blame had to be on him. He was the father. But it had been so hard. Every time he saw his daughter, he thought of his wife, and it was like a searing pain in his chest. He could not have adequately described it to anyone. His sense of loss was so great, he was absolutely crushed. Sometimes the pain was so intense, he literally could not breathe. For months he would break into tears at the oddest things. A scent of her perfume; a remembered joke they shared; walking into an empty house; driving by the school where she taught; a simple song. Anything could set him off. He was despondent, and thoughts of suicide had even entered his mind.

Fortunately, he had good officers working for him who all respected and admired him. At six foot three and almost three hundred pounds, he was one who always seemed to fill a room, and it would be easy for him to have commanded respect. But it was his calm demeanor and kind heart that had won the respect and admiration of his men. They all stepped up and helped him and covered for him. His loss was so great, his grief so overwhelming, he had just not been able to handle knowing his daughter was grieving also. He loved her dearly, and knew she loved him too. But they had always been a threesome. When he had looked at the pain in her heart he felt like he had failed her. And failed his wife. He had taken the job in Sylvester so they could have a simpler, safer life. It had not been safe enough. Somehow, it became his fault, and he could not bear the pain of his loss, much less knowing and feeling the pain he had caused his daughter.

He still had a hard time dealing with it, but time had helped. He now realized that it was not his fault his wife had been killed in the traffic accident. It wasn't his fault, but it was still his loss. Now, he felt guilty about the way he had handled the situation. He had not been there for his daughter, regardless of the reason, and that was wrong. She and her mother had been so close. They shared a bond that was rare between mother and daughter. Not just mutual love, but mutual respect and admiration. A closeness built on many hours spent together in their shared interest in biology, where all problems could be discussed as they went about their work. He knew that Debra had been devastated by her loss, too. He wished they had turned to each other. He even knew it at the time, but he just could not rein in his emotions long enough to deal with it.

Now, time had served to dampen the pain. He still missed his wife, still thought about her every day. But he could be more objective now. He knew his wife would not have been happy with the way he had acted. He missed his daughter. He had called her last night and it had been wonderful. Neither had mentioned their loss. Their conversation was not nearly as strained as it had been. Instead they each talked about their current lives and goings on. She had talked with him about the new job she was starting today. She was excited and proud. And he was excited and proud for her. She had worked hard, and she deserved a great job.

He was also a little worried about his daughter. She had just moved to the suburbs of "Hotlanta," an area he was all too familiar with. He had worked there for many years in his former life as an FBI agent. He knew the area could be fun, exciting and very deadly. Despite their self-anointed slogan as the "city too busy to hate," he knew it might just as appropriately be called "the city too big to care." People just seemed to get swallowed up in the vastness of its nightlife and activities. They got focused on what made them happy and stopped worrying about what was right and good. Crime was rampant, drugs were sold openly on the street corners, and child prostitution was

Fatal Healing

common. Life did not have much value to the gangs of street punks that thrived in the area. Visitors thronged to the city for conventions, ball games and all manner of activities. They did not live there, and had no vested interest in its well-being. It was kind of like driving a rental car. Anything goes. Yes, he was worried about his daughter. And he missed her. He resolved to go see her soon.

The fish were not biting, so he opened his second beer. The last one, he thought. It would not do for the police chief to get caught DUI. He put the beer in a coozie and held it between his feet, as he cast the spinner bait towards the shore. He turned the crank about five turns and a huge bass hit the lure. He set the hook and started trying to reel the bass in, but it took off, peeling line off the reel. He was distracted by movement in the boat and saw that a bream had taken the cricket, and the rod was dancing up and down on the floor of the boat. He reached down to try to grab the rod with the bream, while holding the rod with the bass high in the air and pulling it back to keep the line taut. Just as he touched the rod on the bottom of the boat, the bass turned and jumped with slack in the line, trying to spit the hook. He quickly abandoned his quest for the rod and reeled like crazy trying to keep the fish line taut. He reached out with his foot to secure the rod in the boat, kicking over his beer.

He finally landed the bass, a beauty of about five pounds. The bream had gotten the line wound up in the sunken tree limbs and gotten off. The beer can was empty and his shoes were soaked with the beverage. It was the most fun he had experienced in a year.

-14-

Jack Nebra was totally unprepared for the reaction to his question about balium. Greg Bolin audibly sucked in his breath and sat back in his chair. Tim Murray let out an expletive and also sat back in his chair. Nebra realized he had hit a nerve. Neither man answered his question, so he posed it again, this time to Tim Murray.

"So, what is balium?"

Murray did not look Nebra in the eye. His gaze fixed on the table in front of him. He finally answered. "Balium is a manufactured chemical compound that we use in researching one of our drugs."

"What does it do?" There was silence, and then Greg Bolin answered.

"Look, we can't really talk about this. It is proprietary information. We can't talk about any of our research into new drugs."

Nebra looked at the men and started to say something, then changed his mind. Right now he just wanted information. If he had to, he could play hardball later.

"Was Mr. Windom working with this balium?"

"Yes, he was," answered Bolin.

"Look, guys, let me remind you again. I don't give a rat's butt about what drugs ya'll are researching or making, or whatever. Except when they have a bearing on this case. I have a homicide. Mr. Windom is dead. Now I did not know the man, but you did. He worked with you everyday. It is my job to find out who killed him. That means I have to find out if the man was involved in anything that might have precipitated his death. Now tell me what you can about balium, about what Windom was doing, and if you have any idea why someone would kill the man. You owe him that much, at least."

Murray and Bolin looked at each other. To Nebra, they both looked frightened, and that made him suspicious.

Bolin finally answered. "I will tell you what I can. Gene was working two projects. The first one was trying to find a way to stimulate the re-growth of cartilage. The second was trying to find a cure for the common cold. Probably every company like us has a team working on the same things. That is why we don't talk about our research. Anyway, balium is just a chemical that we use as part of the drug we are making. Gene was the lead researcher on the common cold project. He will be hard to replace, and for that reason, and because we liked him personally, we are sorry he is dead. But we don't know why someone killed him."

Bolin seemed to calm down tremendously as he spoke, and Nebra's suspicion level dropped accordingly.

"How much money did Mr. Windom make?" he asked.

Bolin looked surprised at the change in direction and looked at Murray, who answered. "He made about a hundred and fifty thousand a year, why?"

"Well, he had a really nice house, and he was divorced with two children. That means child support and maybe alimony. He appeared to be doing very well for himself. I was wondering if he might have been selling information about his research to another company and maybe got into a dispute with them."

"I doubt that was the case," said Bolin. "We do a very thorough security check on our people, and we pay them very well. Besides no research material is allowed out of the secured area."

"It was just a thought," said Nebra.

Bolin started to say something, hesitated, then, "Can I ask you something?"

"Sure."

"What made you ask about balium?"

Nebra replied, "Oh, it was just on a piece of scratch paper I found in Windom's house."

"What was on the paper?"

"Well, it was just doodling, but it said 'balium =s SARS', what do you think he meant?" Murray sat back in his chair again, an action that did not go unnoticed by Nebra.

Bolin, though, calmly replied, "Well, SARS is a lot like the common cold. Every drug company is looking for a cure to SARS. He was probably just wondering if our research would let us find it."

Nebra stood up. "Gentlemen, thank you for your time and help. I may need to talk to you again. Meantime, if you think of anything that might help, please call me." He gave each of the men, who were now standing as well, a card.

Murray said, "Thanks. I'll walk down with you."

"I hope you find out who did this," said Bolin. "Gene was a good person."

Nebra shook his hand, and he and Murray left. Bolin went back to his office, stopping just long enough to throw up in the men's bathroom.

♦♦♦

Slaton retrieved the discs he had taken the night before and put them in a briefcase he carried with him to Mr. Wooten's office. When he arrived, the secretary told him to go right in, that Mr. Wooten was expecting him. When he entered the office, Wooten was standing at his large picture window, looking at the Atlanta skyline, hands clasped behind his back. He turned at the sound of Slaton entering the room, and walked back to his desk.

"Have a seat," he told Slaton, as he did so himself. "Tell me everything."

"Well, I went to the house about two. I tried to talk to him so I could find out about the information he had, but he had a gun in his bedside table. He also had a panic button by the bed. When he was getting up, he set the siren off and grabbed the gun. I didn't have a choice, Mr. Wooten. The siren was blasting away, and I knew the cops were coming, so, I couldn't even search the house. I did grab these computer discs, though. Maybe, what you want is on one."

He removed the discs and handed them to Wooten, who regarded them as if they might be contaminated and immediately put them in the floor safe.

"What about the detective?"

"Well, I hadn't been in the office five minutes when he got here. I was about to call you when the security guard at the gate called and told me he was here. Naturally, I met him at the lobby desk and took him back to my office. Windom had his health insurance card in his wallet. It showed he worked here, so the detective came on over. He looked at his personnel file and asked a few general questions. You know, how long he worked here, what he was like, if he had any problems I knew about. That kind of thing. Then he said he wanted to talk to Windom's supervisor. About that time Mr. Murray showed up with the new girl. We called Mr. Bolin, and Mr. Murray took him up to see him. Then, you called. That's it."

Wooten was alarmed. "You mean he is still here? With Bolin and Murray?"

"Well, yes sir. There wasn't really any choice about it, with Murray showing up when he did and all. But I wouldn't worry about it. They can't tell him anything." Wooten sat staring at his security chief, and he did not look well at all. "What about the girl, Ms. Raines? Where was she while all this was going on?"

"Oh, I had her wait in the outer office with Julie, my secretary. When Mr. Murray and the detective left, I called you and then brought her back and gave her the security orientation. She is with officer Billups now, getting the tour and her card and retina scan."

"About last night, are you sure no one saw you? Is there any way someone could put you there?"

"Oh, no, Mr. Wooten. I'm better than that. I was very careful. No one saw me, and there is no trace I was there."

"Okay, Rex. Thanks. You did a good job. I'm sorry you had to kill him, but you had no choice. The man just should not have tried to steal from us and blackmail us. Thanks for taking care of it."

"Well, I'm sorry I couldn't question him, but at least I stopped him."

Windom opened the floor safe and took out an envelope that he passed over to Slaton. "You did a good job, Rex, and I won't forget it."

"What's this, boss?"

"It's a thank you for going above and beyond, Rex. I believe in paying people when they produce results. If Windom had sold that information to another company, it would have cost us a whole lot. And he would have just continued to milk us for a whole lot, to keep him from selling it. I'm sorry he had to die, but, frankly, the S.O.B. had it coming. He was a thief, pure and simple."

Slaton looked in the envelope and saw what had to be at least ten thousand dollars in one hundred dollar bills. "Boss, I can't take this. It's my job to handle security for the company. He was stealing from us, and it was my duty to stop him."

Wooten noted that while Slaton was saying he couldn't accept the money, he was still holding on to it. "Look Rex, this is a bonus for a job well-done. Look at it as that scholarship for your son we talked about. I believe there is just enough to cover about two year's tuition. I'm proud to have a person of your integrity and loyalty working here. Take the money, but don't deposit it. That is cash. Tax-free cash. Don't buy anything big; just use it to cover some of your day-to-day expenses, and a few extras. Rex, you are a good man. I'm proud to have you here. This is a bonus."

With that said, Wooten stood and extended his hand. Rex stood, too, and clasped his boss's hand.

"Thank you, Mr. Wooten. I promise to never let you down."

The door closed behind his security chief, and Jim Wooten turned to the bank of televisions, lost in thought. And, still nervous about what Bolin and Murray might be saying to the detective.

-15-

Mary Hightower and Debra Raines were enjoying a light lunch at Genevieve's, a small local restaurant that specialized in home cooking. They each had decided on a vegetable plate and sweet iced tea with lemon. Debra had learned that Mary was married to the same man for 27 years. She had three children, all married and living in the metro area, and two grandchildren, who were less than a year old. She enjoyed swimming and tennis, and played the latter on an ALTA (Atlanta Lawn Tennis Association) team. She had not attended college, but had graduated from a local technical school, where she had learned office management, typing and other clerical skills. She had been with the Condor Corporation for twelve years and in her current position for seven years. She was very active in the local Christian Church, where her husband, who was a schoolteacher, was a Deacon. She and her husband both sang in the choir, and she taught a women's Bible study. Her husband used to teach, also, but decided teaching five days a week was plenty. He taught advanced mathematics at a large private school called Woodward Academy, and was looking forward to retirement in another five years. They lived in Villa Rica, which was just west of Douglasville. Mary had about a fifteen-minute drive to work, but her husband, Dan, had a good thirty to forty minute commute. They built their new home two years ago in the country and loved it. Her children always kidded them about building a home twice as big as the one they had when the children were all at home. It didn't make sense until you thought about three families visiting at once, she remarked.

Mary had learned about Debra's college degree and her basketball and track participation. She learned about Debra's mother, and what a terrific lady she had been, and about the tragic accident that had ended her life. She learned about her father, the police chief, and about the small town of Sylvester. She, having learned that Debra was single and not seeing anyone, immediately started thinking about young men with whom she could fix her up. She invited Debra to church, and secured a promise from her that she would visit this coming Sunday.

It was an easy and comfortable conversation for them both. Mary took an instant liking to this striking young girl who was the same age as her daughter. Her home had always been the hang out for her children's friends. With two boys and a girl, it seemed the house was always over-flowing. The kids all seemed to like her, and she had earned the nickname "other mother" from a few. Debra could see personality traits that reminded her of her mother and felt a bond with Mary that was far stronger than the hour's time they had known each other would normally warrant.

They paid their bill and got back into Mary's car for the short drive back to work. For the first time, the conversation turned to the Condor Corporation.

"When I was waiting in the lobby this morning, I saw all of the pictures of Mr. Wooten with the President and other important people, as well as the awards. Pretty impressive. And he certainly seems to be polished man. In fact, I was impressed with Mr. Horton, and Mr. Murray too. Especially Mr. Murray. He looks like he stepped out of GQ magazine, and he was very well spoken."

"Oh yes, there is no doubt about it. They are all smart. Even though I have been with the company a long time, I rarely see Mr. Wooten. He's gone a lot of the time, and the building is so big. Plus, we aren't exactly in the same social circle. And I've only seen Mr. Horton in the elevator or at the company Christmas party, but I see Mr. Murray fairly often. With him being the personnel vice president, I guess he just naturally makes himself more visible to the employees. Plus, he and Mr. Bolin, our boss, are pretty good friends. They play racquetball sometimes at lunch. It really is a good place to work. The people are all nice, and it's exciting to know that we are developing treatments that could cure people. My mother died of breast cancer, and I'm always hoping that someone in our company will actually find the cure. We have a good team of people trying, and they have already developed some treatments that have had fairly good success. Maybe that's the team you will work on," Mary said, as she turned and smiled at Debra.

"Maybe. I'm kind of anxious and a little scared to find out exactly what I'll be doing. I hope I'm not a disappointment. I want to do well here. I like the people I have met so far, and the area, too."

"Don't worry, Debra. I'm sure you will do well. One of the guys described the work as a lot like deep-sea fishing. He said it can be very boring at times, but there is always anticipation about what might happen, and when you get a bite, it's instant gratification. I wouldn't know about that. My work is pretty mundane, but when we are getting close to a big cure, like Cold-X, even I get excited."

"Yeah, they mentioned that in the meeting this morning. That's a project I would like to work on," Debra said as Mary parked the car.

"Well, maybe you will. I guess you will know in a few minutes," she said as the women started into the lobby.

The receptionist greeted them with a smile and said, "I see they got you all fixed up," pointing at Debra's ID Badge.

"They sure did. Now, I get to find out what I'll be working on," Debra said, smiling.

The receptionist waved at them as she answered the telephone. "Condor Corporation. How may I direct your call?"

Mary and Debra waved back and got on the elevator. "I really enjoyed lunch, Mary. Thank you so much for showing me that restaurant. I am so tired of fast food. Let's go again sometime soon. Next time, I'll drive."

"I'd like that," said Mary. "If I'm going to go in that little car, though, you'll have to let the top down."

"Deal. It is really a fun car to drive. You'll see," said Debra, as the elevator door opened, and they stepped into the hallway. The two women walked the rest of the way in comfortable silence, each wondering where Debra would be working and with whom.

-16-

Jack Nebra left the Condor Corporation and stopped for a chicken sandwich, to go. He called Detective Joel Smith and talked to him for a few minutes. After reviewing the information they each had, they decided to meet at the coroner's office. Jack arrived first at the one story brick front building and waited.

The building was in an area of combined warehouse and office space. It had fairly large windows and a double glass door in the front of the brick veneer. A green canopy over the front door accented the red brick. From the front, it looked like a very nice office building. There were no ambulances or hearses visible to change that impression. The building appeared to be offices for a successful business, perhaps a doctor or lawyer or accountant. A view from the side and rear showed the building was actually a large warehouse with loading docks at the rear. The coroner's official sedan and two specially equipped and unmarked Chevrolet Tahoes were kept in the rear. The dark blue, matching Tahoes had tinted windows and had been stripped of their seats. They were equipped with a metal stainless steel floor and two gurneys each. The gurneys were on wheels, and there were straps built into the floor to secure them. They served only one purpose - to transport bodies as unobtrusively as possible. There was no life saving equipment, no sirens, no police lights. The occupants of these gurneys were always long past needing any of these things.

The building was built as it was for very good reasons. It was designed so that deceased relatives would not feel like they were entering a cold, antiseptic morgue where bodies were stored in a refrigerated room in stainless steel drawers with tags on their toes. In fact, bodies were stored in just such a manner, but the relatives never saw that. Instead, they entered a normal business office, where a secretary greeted them. There was a small, simple prayer room, so marked by a small plaque beside the door, on the left side of the waiting room. When the identification was to be made, the visitors were escorted down a hall to a small conference room, where the body was located. Their escort was a calm, well-dressed county employee trained to deal with a wide range of emotions. On many occasions a police representative also accompanied them; a detective in the event of a crime, or an officer in the event the death was traffic related.

Detective Smith arrived and parked next to Nebra. The men got out and walked into the building. Neither were strangers here, and they waved to the secretary and proceeded into the hallway and through a door that visitors never entered. From there they went into an area where there were two bathrooms and storage shelves containing plastic booties and aprons. They each donned these garments and proceeded through another hermetically sealed stainless steel door. Nebra was always impressed with the kind and considerate way in which the next of kin were treated here. He was glad they did not ever have to see the area he and his partner had just entered. They were in the morgue itself, and the smell of formaldehyde and body fluids mingled together in an unforgettable and very unpleasant manner.

The floor was concrete that had been painted and sealed with many coats of paint. There were floor drains every ten feet or so, and water hoses were coiled neatly against the walls for later use in scrubbing the floors. The two detectives were glad for the protection offered by the booties and apron. The floor, although washed several times a day by prison labor, was stained with blood and was tacky in some areas as they walked toward the workstations. The room was frigid cold, and the men each wanted a coat. Giant ventilators hummed as they worked ineffectively to cleanse the air of odor.

While many of the bodies that entered here were later transferred to funeral homes for the embalming process, some were not. One such body lay on one of the embalming tables now - a "floater" or drowning victim, it appeared from its bloated, washed out condition. The person had not been identified and would be embalmed here before getting a pauper's burial, if that remained the case.

There were several workstations in the area, each with stainless steel beds sloped in a manner that allowed all body fluids to drain into collection points. There were large bright overhead lights and instrument tables for surgical tools. Except for the special beds and the scales and instruments used to weigh and measure body parts, the workstations resembled an ordinary operating room. It was at one of these stations they saw Doctor Jesus Chavez, Chief Coroner for Douglas County. He looked up and motioned the men over with a gloved hand.

He was working on a black female of about thirty. She was emaciated looking and her arms were filled with needle marks that appeared white against the bloodless skin - another victim of the drugs so prevalent in her society. There is no dignity in death. The girl's naked body was on her back, and she was cut in an x pattern that exposed all of her organs. Nebra wondered again about those that would not be organ donors because they did not want their bodies violated. They wanted to be buried with their bodies as God made them. Sorry. When the autopsy was finished, the parts might go back into the corpse, but not in any manner God would recognize. Bolin knew of times when tongues had to be cut off and mouths and eyelids sewn shut so the body would seem "natural." He was saddened by the unnatural death that surrounded him. He did not enjoy this part of his job, but it did serve to feed his determination to find those responsible for the crimes that caused this destruction.

"Hello, Doctor Chavez. It looks like you've found another victim of the streets."

"Yeah, it's called job security. What with the accidental deaths, the murders and these senseless drug deaths, I will never be out of work."

"Drug overdose?"

"More like drug over use. She just abused her body so much that it shut down. It wasn't the last dose that got her; it was all the ones she had before. What a waste. There is no telling the number of people that were hurt and abused by her life and death."

"Doc, you obviously haven't heard. Drug use is a victimless crime. The only ones hurt are the ones that use them."

Doctor Chavez gave a short laugh. "Right, and God was a comedian. I guess you are here about last night's homicide victim. Come on. I want to show you something."

He turned out the overhead lights that had so glaringly illuminated the girl's body, and led them to another station. He switched on the overhead lights of this station and pointed to Gene Windom's chest. Three bullet holes, in a tight pattern, penetrated the man's body just to the right of the left breast. Nebra and Smith looked at the body and immediately knew what Doctor Chavez was alluding to. A professional had shot this man. Whoever the killer was, he had certainly had training in firing a weapon. Three closely grouped shots like that were the mark of a true sharpshooter. Military shooters and cops were trained to fire in quick three shot bursts. Very few people were as good as this shooter.

Chavez said: "Two of the bullets penetrated the heart, and the third just missed it. The guy was dead before his head hit the floor."

Nebra and Smith looked at each other. This was an interesting development. It was one thing to think a random thief looking for drug money or something had killed the man. It was quite another to find the man had been killed by a professional caliber shooter. This was looking like a contract killing, not a random robbery gone bad. They thanked Doctor Chavez and left the building.

Both men breathed deeply of fresh air as they walked toward their cars.

"Joel, I don't think that I will ever get used to that. I don't know how Doc does that day after day."

"I asked him that once," said Detective Smith. "He told me he told himself that at least these people would suffer no more. Their time of violence and pain was over. He didn't understand how we dealt with the on-going violence and senseless harm that continues on a day-to-day basis. I guess we each do what we can. But I'm with you. If nothing else, I could just not handle that smell all the time. Where to now?"

"I think we need to go back to the deceased's house. I want to look at it again now that it appears he was an intentional and not a random victim."

"Yeah, me too. I'll meet you there."

The men got into their respective cars and started out, Nebra leading the way. They each mulled over the things they learned this day, as they traveled the ten or so miles back to

Gene Windom's house. They parked in front and ducked under the police tape that was still surrounding the scene. The locks had been changed, and there was a lock box on the door. Detective Smith entered his personal code in the box, and it opened. He withdrew the key and the men entered the house.

It was odd, entering a stranger's house, knowing that only a short time earlier, another stranger had entered this same door and taken the owner's life. There was dead silence, and the men found themselves talking in muted tones. They started at the front door, and Jack showed Detective Smith the residue of duct tape on the doorframe that had been photographed earlier. Both men knew the tape had likely held a magnet in place that circumvented the house security system. They then moved methodically from room to room, looking for any clue that would help them solve this murder. They and others had already done this once, but sometimes a second look produced results - especially once other information had been obtained that caused you to have a more discerning eye.

They next went to the bedroom where the deceased was found. Jack tried to picture the scene in his mind. How exactly had it happened? Windom had obviously gotten out of bed and hit the panic button on the wall beside the door. Had he gotten up because he heard something, or had he gotten up because he was told to? If it were a professional, the way they were thinking now, Jack doubted he had made much, if any, noise. But if the killer were standing in front of him with a gun, it was pretty gutsy to hit the panic button and grab a gun. That is, unless he figured he was going to die anyway. And if he knew he was going to die, he probably had done something that would give someone reason to kill him. What could a man, who seemingly had it all together, have done to provoke someone enough to kill him?

Jack thought about the close pattern of bullet's holes in Windom's chest. There was no way a shooter could have done that on the move. He had to be standing, poised and ready to fire. So, he was probably already in the room, and ordered Windom up. Also, there would have to have been good light for him to be that accurate. More light than would have come around the window curtains at that hour of morning. He made a note to ask the first officer on the scene whether the overhead light had been on or off when they found the body.

Next, they entered the bathroom, but each detective knew there was nothing here. The crime had taken place in the bedroom. Neither the killer nor the deceased had made it this far into the master bathroom. But, they had to look. Jack noted again the orderliness of the closet and bath area, and the men moved back through the bedroom to the living room. Had the killer entered the foyer and moved straight back to the bedroom? There was nothing here that would tell them anything. Next was the kitchen/ dining area. Jack noted again the half bottle of scotch. If Windom had many of those, he probably would have been sleeping too soundly to hear an intruder. Especially one that knew what he was doing. He made a note to check with Doctor Chavez about the blood-alcohol content of the deceased.

They moved on to the office. There was a computer desk and a nice Dell computer, a small sofa, some framed photographs. The usual reams of paper were on a shelf above the printer. A modern, flat screen eighteen-inch monitor, some books and not much else. This room, too, reflected Windom's cleanliness and neat nature. Jack turned to leave, and then turned back and took one last look around.

The men locked up the house, made a date to meet at the office in the morning, and each turned their cars toward home. It had been a long day.

-17-

Greg Bolin had never felt so washed out. He was young and healthy and athletic and brilliant. Right now he felt like an old man who not only was physically weak, but whose thoughts were fuzzy. Taking the balium to China was one thing; he did not know those people, had no connections to them and looked at the deaths that resulted from the SARS epidemic as justifiable. After all, once Cold-X was available, many more lives would be saved than were lost. It was truly a case of the ends justifying the means. They all agreed to that, and he had convinced himself it was true.

But Gene Windom was different. He was a co-worker; someone he had known and worked with for years. And he knew that Gene's death had not been a random home invasion turned murder. It was murder, pure and simple. And, it was a murder that would probably haunt them with its repercussions. He had not known anything about the home invasion and murder until Tim Murray had called him, but he was not much of a believer in coincidence. He had not arranged for Windom to die, but he was pretty sure who did. He drank deeply from the water cooler, trying to clear his head. Then, he went into his office and called Mr. Wooten.

"We need to talk," he said when his boss answered the phone, his voice stronger than he felt.

"Yes, we do. This is an interesting development. Call Murray and Bill Horton, and let's meet at two o'clock, here in my office."

Bolin looked at his watch. It was only one fifteen.

"Okay. You know that Windom is dead, and a detective has been here?"

"I know. Save it. We'll talk when you get here," Wooten said, hanging up the phone without further comment.

Bolin looked at the receiver in his hand and shook his head, "interesting development? That's not exactly how I would have put it," he thought. He called Bill Horton.

"We are supposed to meet in Mr. Wooten's office at two. Windom's dead," he said, without preamble.

The accountant was stunned. "Dead! What do you mean? How was he killed? What is going on?"

"I don't know anything except that someone apparently broke into his home and killed him. We'll talk about it at two. I have to go. Bye."

Bolin hung up the phone. He was glad Horton was upset. He really did not care for Horton. He dressed like a slob, and Bolin thought he was mousy. "Let him sweat for a while, too," he thought.

He called to tell Murray about the meeting, but his secretary said he was not in. He left word for him to call him as soon as possible and hung up, just as the man walked into his office, unannounced.

"Damn, Greg, I don't like this at all," said Murray, as he sat down in one of the chairs in front of Bolin.

"Hey, Tim. I just tried to call you. We're supposed to meet with Wooten at two. I don't like this either."

Murray looked at his watch. "What do you make of it? Who do you think killed Windom?"

Bolin sighed. He was feeling a little better, but not perfect. "Tim, I just don't know. I'm scared to death. The last thing we need is to have the cops snooping around, asking questions like, 'What's balium?'"

"I know. But we didn't kill him. I don't know anything that we can do but cooperate."

The intercom on Bolin's desk came on. "Mr. Bolin, I'm back from lunch, and Ms. Raines is here. Do you have a minute?" Mary Hightower asked.

Bolin rolled his eyes and looked at Tim Murray. "Just what I need right now. Dealing with a new hire with all of this going on."

"Yeah, well, I'll let you get to it. See you at two." Tim Murray rose to leave, and Bolin came around the desk and walked him to the door.

"Okay," he said opening the door.

Debra Raines stood up when the men came out of the inner office and smiled at them.

"Hello, again," she said to Tim Murray.

"Hello, Ms. Raines. Let me introduce you to your boss. This is Greg Bolin. Greg, this is Debra Raines."

The two shook hands, and Murray said, "I'll see you in a little while, Greg. Ms Raines, good luck. I know you will like it here."

Bolin gave a short wave to his friend and asked Debra to come into his office. She sat in the chair just vacated and smiled across the desk at her new boss.

"May I call you Debra?" He asked.

"Yes, please do."

"Good. And I am Greg. We will all be working too close together to be too formal. Debra, I'm afraid there has been a tragedy that has me a little upset, and that requires my attention. I won't be able to give you the time you deserve right now, and I apologize for it. Normally, I would take you around to meet everyone and show you where you will be working, but I just can't do that right now. Let me talk to you for a few minutes, and then I will get Mary to take you around and do that. I take it that you and Mary have already gotten to know each other?"

"Oh, yes sir, we have. We had lunch together. She's terrific. And you do what you need to and don't worry about me."

"Thanks, I appreciate that. I've read your resumé. It is quite impressive. And I saw from the security clearance report, that you are a native Georgian. Sylvester, I believe. That's down between Tifton and Albany, isn't it?"

"Yes, that's right. I was actually born in Atlanta, but we moved there when I was very small."

"I was down in that area once when I went dove hunting on one of the plantations in the area. It's beautiful country."

Debra laughed. "Yes sir, it is beautiful, and it's definitely country. Life moves at a whole different pace down there."

"Debra, we have a lot of different projects going on. Being new, you will have a pretty good learning curve to go through anyway, so I thought I would let you get an overview of the different projects and see if there is one that really grabs your attention. If there is, we'll plug you in there. It will be a lot more fun if there is one that really interests you. At first, of course, you'll mostly be doing grunt work until you get a good feel for the project. How does that sound?"

"That sounds great to me, sir. I'm excited to just have this opportunity. Put me wherever you like, and I will do my best."

"Okay, good. I'll get Mary to take you around and introduce you to the different project heads, and they can tell you a little about what they are working on. Ask them questions, now, so you'll know where you want to work."

He pushed the button on his intercom and asked Mary to come in. His secretary immediately opened the door.

"Yes sir?"

"Come in, Mary. Have a seat. I need you to do something for me. We have had a tragedy, and I have some things that I just have to do. I need you to take Debra around to the different project heads and introduce her to the people. Let her find out a little about each project, and we'll see what interests her. I may as well tell you what is going on, because you will know soon enough."

He paused for a moment. He felt much better now that his mind had been occupied with something other than the murder, but he knew he would be thinking of little else for a while, and he was not looking forward to that.

"Gene Windom was killed last night in a home invasion. The police have already been here getting information about him as part of their routine investigation. I really don't know any more than that right now. You may as well let the others know. I'll let everyone know about the arrangements as soon as I find out."

Mary Hightower sat with her hand to her mouth and tears in her eyes. Gene Windom had been her friend, as well as her co-worker. They worked together for many years. He had sought her advice while he was going through his divorce, and they became good friends. He had even come to her church for a while. Her preacher had been very supportive and had tried to help Gene and his wife work things out. She could not believe the man was dead. She had just seen him the day before yesterday.

"Oh, no," she said now. "That is terrible. He was such a good man. And his poor kids. I just can't believe it."

"Yes, I know. It hit me hard, too. I guess none of us ever knows when our time will come. Debra, I'm sorry that this happened on your first day. Gene was my chief researcher. Among other things, he was the chief of the Cold-X project."

"I'm so sorry," said Debra. "But don't worry about me. Ya'll do what you need to."

Mary had tears rolling down her cheek as she spoke. "Boss, I don't know how this is going to work. I can't very well say: 'This is Debra Raines, she is going to be working with us, and, by the way, Gene Windom was killed last night!' How can I handle this?"

Bolin looked at his secretary for a moment and said, "Of course you are right, Mary. That just won't work. That would not be fair to anyone. I should have given this more thought. I'm just not thinking clearly." He thought for a moment and turned to Debra.

"Ms. Raines, I am so sorry that this has happened. I know you were looking forward to starting today, and we were looking forward to that as well. But under the circumstances, I think it would be better if we let you start tomorrow. That way, we can let people know about Gene. In fact, tomorrow is Friday, and I am sure we will all be dealing with this tomorrow too. Why don't you plan on starting to work Monday, instead? Your pay will still start today. I'm really sorry this has happened, but I think it would be best if we do it that way. What do you think, Mary?"

"Oh yes sir. That would be so much better. That way, we will all have the weekend to get used to this. Please, let's do it that way."

"Is that okay with you Debra?" he asked, turning back to her.

"Whatever you say, sir. I think it would be better that way. I really don't want to be thought of as the girl who started the day Gene was killed."

"Okay, let's do that. You go on and try not to think about this. We'll see you Monday morning," he said standing and offering his hand.

Debra stood and shook the outstretched hand. She told Mary she would see her Sunday, and left. Mary had taken a Kleenex from the box on her boss's desk and sat dabbing at her eyes, trying not to smear makeup all over her face.

"I still can't believe this, Greg. I just can't."

"I know, Mary. I can't either. But I have to go now. Stay here as long as you need to. Once you feel like you are up to it, please let the others know."

"Yes sir, I will. Thank you."

Greg Bolin walked around his desk and patted his secretary on the shoulder. There was really nothing left to say. He left her in his office as he went to meet with Mr. Wooten.

◆◆◆

Bill Horton sat fretting at his desk. Gene Windom was dead. He did not know the man, and his thoughts were not about Windom, but about how this death would affect him. In one way, it solved their immediate problem about him blackmailing them. It would have cost him big bucks to put up his share of the money to bring Windom into the loop. So, in that regard, he was glad the man was dead. Adios. But, what if the investigation into his murder led back to them? He wondered if Windom had left anything around that would cause them problems. He wondered who had killed Windom. Was it one of the other three, or had one hired it done, or was it a random event totally unrelated to this Cold-X thing? If one of the others had him killed, that would mean still another person outside the loop was now involved. What problems would that cause? He wondered about these things a lot. In fact, he could think of little else, until time came for him to go to Mr. Wooten's office.

♦♦♦

Tim Murray returned to his office, got the message to call Greg Bolin, tossed it in the trash and paced back and forth in his office. Gene Windom's death had caught him by surprise, and it was obvious that it had surprised Greg, too. He discounted the possibility that his death was really just a random event as being too great a coincidence. That left Horton and Wooten, which really just left Wooten. Horton did not have the nerve to do anything like that. Mr. Wooten, on the other hand, would. He knew that Wooten could be ruthless, and he would not have taken being blackmailed lightly. He also knew that Wooten would not have done the deed himself. In fact, he probably was somewhere where he had a great alibi, unlike the rest of us, he thought. But if he had hired the killing out, whom would he have chosen? And how could he be sure of that person's silence?

He had no doubt that Wooten had taken every precaution he could to protect himself and their little project. He was brilliant. He was also a survivor; something they all needed to remember. If things went well, Wooten would do just exactly what he said he would do, and they would all be rich. But if things went south, he would not hesitate to hang them all out to dry if it would help his case. Murray did not like the idea of bringing Windom into the deal, and he surely resented the idea of paying the man some of the money that would have been his own. But he did not like the idea of murdering him, either. Specifically, he acknowledged to himself, he did not like the idea that murdering him would somehow cause their scheme to be exposed and bring them all down. He really did not have a problem with Windom's death. After all, he barely knew the man.

Well, he thought, we are in it now. If Windom had lived, he could have continued to blackmail them, so it was better that he was dead. In the unlikely event it was a true home invasion and killing, then it would just end at that. The note about "Balium =s SARS" was easily enough explained the way Greg had done for the detective. Just random thoughts about how we might be able to cure the problem. The detective did not know squat about their research. If Wooten had ordered the hit, then he would just have to trust the man had it done in such a manner that they would not come under suspicion. He had a lot of confidence in his boss. He looked at his watch, smiled, and left for the meeting.

Fatal Healing

-18-

Rex Slaton left Wooten's office and went back to his own. Once there, he asked not to be disturbed and took out the envelope of money that Wooten had given him. He counted the money. Fifteen thousand dollars! Rex did not know whether to laugh or cry. That was more money than he had seen all at once in his whole life. Oh, sure, he and his wife made a decent living. But it took just about everything they made to pay bills, and they had very little savings. He had more than that in his 401k, but that wasn't money he could really use. A part of him disliked that Wooten had given him the money. It made Windom's death like a contract killing, and that wasn't it at all. The man had been stealing information from the company and trying to blackmail his boss. It had been his job as Chief of Security to try and handle that problem. The man had gotten killed because he was doing wrong, pure and simple. But he was sure grateful for the money. He was going to look at it as a bonus, and he sure wasn't going to give it back.

He put the money in his pocket and left for lunch. He told his secretary he was not planning to come back because he had been there until two the night before. If there was a problem, he could be reached on his cell phone. Then he went to a nearby sports bar where he had chicken wings and beer.

Rex Slaton was not a brilliant man, and he knew that. He made up for it by being strong and loyal, and even brave, as shown by his military record. He had risen to sergeant in the police force partly because he was likable, partly because of his loyalty to his superiors and mostly because he simply out lasted the other officers. They either quit police work entirely or transferred to other departments outside of Fulton County, where the pay was better and the danger level was lower. But loyal Rex just stayed right there. He would have still been there had it not been for the excessive force charges. Jim Wooten had taken Rex in when he was down, and was now the recipient of Rex's fast loyalty.

That did not mean that Rex understood everything his boss said. The part about how to use this cash had gone right over his head, probably because he had been too busy looking at the money. He finished his lunch and drove to his house where he parked his sedan and got into his small Toyota truck. Rex and his wife had made a decent life for their family, but there was no money for many extras. And he wanted a fishing boat. He always had. He dreamed of it. He and his son had fished from the banks of the river on many occasions, and he had always envied those fishermen with boats who could so easily get to those places he could not.

He and his son had often talked about how good it would be to have a small fishing boat, and had stopped by Shamrock

Marine and looked at them on several occasions. In fact, just two weeks ago they stopped by and looked. There was a beautiful blue fiberglass one with an 80 horsepower outboard and a trolling motor they agreed would be perfect for them. Perfect except for the ten thousand dollar price tag.

As Rex drove to the boat dealership, he thought of how excited his son would be. He knew Mr. Wooten had said something about this money being like a college scholarship, but this was better. His son would probably get a football scholarship, anyway. This boat would give them the opportunity to do more things together and bond before he did go off to school, and that was a good thing. Besides, he would still have five thousand dollars. He promised himself he would put that money aside for the college fund.

It was about a thirty-minute drive to the boat dealership. The time passed quickly for Rex, because his mind was already imagining the fun he and his son would have. Heck, they might just load it up and go camping on the river this weekend. They would float and fish until they got tired, find a nice bank and camp out; then get up at daybreak when the fish were really biting, and they would already be there. No driving to the river and hiking down the bank to a good spot. Just get up and get in the boat and go. Rex was a very happy and excited man.

When he arrived at the dealership and parked, the salesmen did not even bother to come out to meet him. They were used to him coming and looking around with his son, and they knew he was a looker, not a buyer. He fooled them today, though. Rex walked over to the blue Glastron and walked slowly around it, looking for flaws. There were a few scratches here and there he might even be able to rub out, but that was it. The boat appeared to be in great shape. He looked at the live well, at the prop and the small trolling motor. He took so much time that finally one of the newer salesmen ambled over to him.

"She's a real beauty, ain't she?"

"Yeah, she is. What's the story on her."

"Well, from what I understand, we sold this boat new to an old guy about five years ago. He lived over in Villa Rica. He died recently, and his daughter brought the boat over here for us to tune it up so she could sell it, and we just bought it from her. This thing probably didn't get used five times a year, she said. He kept it in the carport and would go out and wash it from time to time, but it got to be too much trouble for him to hook it up and all. It's the best deal on the lot."

"What's the least you'll take for her?"

"Well, they want ten thousand for the boat. And that's a bargain. I don't think they'll take any less. The only reason to sell it at that price is cause we have so much inventory. That, and we got it for such a good deal."

"Well, I want to buy the boat, and I'm not saying she isn't worth that much money, but that's a little more than I can afford. I'm willing to go nine thousand though."

"Oh, man, you are killing me. My sales manager will throw me out of his office, if I take him an offer like that. How about ninety-eight hundred dollars?"

"Look, I'll pay ninety-five hundred, but that's it. Not a penny more.

"Well, I'll take it to him, but don't get your hopes up. I think we've already turned that much down. This is a good boat. Come on, let's go inside, and I'll see what I can do for you."

They went inside the showroom, which was loaded with big, new, watercraft. The smell of new gel coat permeated the air. It was wonderful. Any other time, Rex would have been content to just meander around and look and smell that smell. But today, he was a buyer. He was so excited, he could not keep still. He rubbed his head, his arms, his neck. He paced. He did not want to sit down, and he did not want the blue fishing boat to be out of sight. The salesman went to talk with a man that must have been the sales manager, because Rex could see them talking and gesturing at the Glastron. He wandered about the showroom looking at the magnificent boats. He stopped and was looking at a brand new fishing rig with a two hundred horsepower motor and every extra a fisherman could want, when the salesman came up to him.

"Man, I can't believe it. You must have caught him at a really good time, 'cause he said all right. Let's go write it up."

They walked back to the salesman's office. It was a cubicle of about five feet by five feet with a small desk and a couple of chairs in front of it. The salesman started filling out the sales sheet, filling in the serial numbers and ID numbers of the boat, the motor and the trailer. He got the information from a large black book filled with photographs of all of the boats in stock. He then left Rex alone for a few minutes, while he went out to the boat and double-checked all the numbers. Rex didn't mind.

He was too busy thinking about how excited and surprised his son would be.

"Okay, here it is. Just sign on that bottom line. You can give me a five hundred dollar deposit to hold the boat until you get back from the bank, if you need to. You can take this with you when you go. You'll need it when you borrow the money. We'll have her all cleaned up for you when you get back."

"That's okay. I've got the money with me. Tell them to clean it up now, 'cause I'm taking her home!"

The salesman did not miss a beat. He used the phone and called someone to clean up the boat and turned back to Rex, who was looking over the paperwork and not looking very happy at all.

"What are all these charges?" Rex said pointing at several pre-printed amounts on the form.

"Oh, those are standard fees. Everybody has to pay them. This seventy -five dollar charge is for all the paperwork we have to do to get you title to the boat. You have to have that. We only charge what it costs us. The two hundred and fifty dollar dealer prep is standard too. Every dealership charges one. That pays for getting the boat ready and all kinds of things. Probably for the boss to go out to dinner," he winked, "but, it's a standard fee. And the last one is the sales tax. You know the government always gets their part. Can't be helped. Gotta pay that too. But man, you got the best deal I've seen since I've been here."

There were actually two or three other nickel and dime charges that Rex suspected were just add-ons, but it was too late. He had to have the boat, and he had to drive it home. And even the novice salesman knew that was the case. Rex sighed and signed the documents. He pulled out the envelope and counted out the ten thousand six hundred dollars and change. The salesman did not even blink. It was like this type of transaction happened every day. He took the money and returned about fifteen minutes later with a receipt and bill of sale for the boat. They went out to hook up the boat trailer. Rex noted the "clean-up" amounted to rinsing the boat off with a water hose. Fortunately all the trailer lights worked, and Rex Slaton drove off. He was the proud owner of a nice fishing boat. The previous nights events seemed a distant memory.

-19-

J ack Nebra returned to his apartment after a long nine hours
on duty for the Douglas County police department. The
thought of having a drink to unwind briefly crossed his mind,
but with a sense of accomplishment and satisfaction, he
dismissed the thought. Ten years earlier and fresh out of
college, Jack had been a rising star at the FBI. In college he
had excelled in classes, while still managing to party-and drink-
virtually every night. He had continued this behavior after
graduation. In college, he attended three to four classes a day,
but never before nine, and then completed his studying in the
afternoon and early evening. By ten he was done, wired and
ready for another night. Unfortunately, real life did not work
that way. As an FBI agent he had to be at work by seven and
rarely got home before six. He was on call often.

Jack would not have lasted eight years with the FBI, if it
were not for partners who covered for him and his natural
ability as an investigator. His name helped, too, as his father
had been a career FBI agent of high rank and reputation.
Despite good and sometimes brilliant work, the life that Jack

was burning at both ends caught up with him. After five years on the job, he was put on probation for "unprofessional behavior". Translated that meant that Jack had come to work while on call and had reported inebriated. It was not a pleasant memory - for him, for his partner, or for those around them. He was smart enough to lay off the partying for a while until things went back to normal and memories of the embarrassment had dimmed. However, two more episodes, though minor to the first one, sealed his dismissal. Looking back, Jack realized it might have been the best thing to ever happen to him. He finally faced his problem and, with the help of a program at his new church, had not had a drink in over two years. He was hired by the Douglas County Police Force about a year and a half ago, after a recommendation from his church pastor and an FBI friend of the Chief. So far, it was a perfect match. The force benefited from Jack's advanced training by the FBI, and Jack enjoyed the low-pressure atmosphere that allowed him reasonably good hours.

Jack looked around the neat, modern one bedroom apartment and decided the best way to relax would be a couple of laps in the apartment pool. He thought about supper and decided he would take a swim first and worry about that later. He put on his bathing suit, a polo shirt, and a pair of sandals, put a load of clothes in the wash, and grabbed a towel. He was out the door and headed for the pool within two minutes.

Jack's apartment was on ground level and was less than two hundred feet from the pool. Occasionally, the noise from this area could be disturbing, but in Jack's mind, the view of the pool, and the abundance of young women working on their tan, far outweighed any disadvantage. He entered the gate and was greeted by a chorus of other residents. Jack had made many acquaintances and even a few friends since moving to the SunDown Apartments when he took the job with the police force. At six foot one and two hundred pounds, Jack was an imposing man. There was no fat on his muscular body. He had close cropped, thick brown hair and green eyes and a chiseled face that women found intriguing and men found a little threatening.

"Hey, Jen, Mike. Mind if I take this chair?" Jack asked, as he put his towel down on one of the colorful vinyl lounge chairs.

"Hey, yourself," Mike answered.

Jen opened her eyes and shielded the sun with her hand.

"Hey Jack, the sun's still good, join us." she smiled.

Jack spread out his towel and stripped off his shirt to the admiring looks of several women around the pool.

"Thanks, I think I'll take a swim first and work out a few kinks. I've been on my feet all day, it seems," Jack said.

He dove into the Olympic-sized pool and swam under water for most of its length. Surfacing, he swam freestyle to the far end, flipped and swam back. Jack was a strong swimmer. His strokes were long and smooth, and he raced through the water with what appeared to be little effort. He reached the end, took another lap doing the breast-stroke, and then came back free-style again.

Jack's exercise was watched intently by several of the young people around the pool. Most of the guys were a little envious.

Most of the girls were appraising. He exited the pool and dried the water from his tingling skin.

"Wow, the water is still a little chilly when you first get in!" He exclaimed.

"I know, I like it that way. In another month it will be like bathwater, and I hate that," said Mike.

"It sure makes the sun feel good," Jack said. "I think I'll soak up a few rays." He turned the lounge chair so that it faced the sun and stretched out.

"You are late getting here today," Mike commented. "Did you have a rough day protecting us from the 'crumminals?' " he asked, intentionally mispronouncing the word.

Jack closed his eyes. "Something like that." He then briefly told them about the robbery and murder on which he had been working.

"I really can't tell you too much, since it is an on-going investigation, but it may be a case of forced entry and home robbery that went wrong, or perhaps something more. The intruder or intruders might not have known anyone would be at home. The victim actually got out of bed and set off the burglar alarm. He had a pistol, but never got the chance to use it."

"That's terrible," exclaimed Jen. "You said 'they.' How many were there?"

"Oh, we don't know that for sure. It could have been just one. The victim was shot multiple times. I guess it won't hurt to tell you. It will be in all the papers anyway. He was a research assistant at the Condor Corporation."

◆◆◆

Debra Raines was experiencing a range of emotions. Her first day at work had not gone at all as expected. She was impressed with everyone and everything she had seen, but the murder business had really thrown a damper on things. She had not expected to be sent home like some child on her first day at work, but she knew that was really the best alternative. It just wasn't in any scenarios she had imagined about her first day. Now, she had tomorrow and the whole weekend. She thought briefly about going home to Sylvester to see her father, but decided she had too much to do to get settled in her new apartment. She drove past the SunDown apartments and turned into WindSong Townhomes, where she had rented a two bedroom just four days earlier. She had decided on these apartments because there were some garages, and she was able to rent one for her new car. But they were at the end of the building, so for now, she parked in front of B-12 and locked her car.

Debra's apartment had a floor plan similar to many others she had looked at. Someone had told her they were "cookie-cutter" apartments, because they all looked the same. The downstairs consisted of a small, but modern, kitchen, a dining room and living room in an L shape, a half bath and a small screen porch at the rear. If you stood on the porch, as Debra was now, you could look to your far right and see a portion of the pool and clubhouse. The upstairs of her apartment had two fairly good-sized bedrooms, each with its own bathroom. The apartment had new carpet, and the appliances were in good shape. It was also Debra's first apartment, and the first time she had lived by herself. Compared to the dorm rooms she had become used to, it was a mansion. Her father would choke if he knew how much the rent was.

She thought briefly of going to the pool, but decided to use her time more wisely and see if she could finish hanging pictures and unpacking. She really did not have that much left to do, and she was finished before time for supper. She had only stopped at the grocery long enough to buy the essentials, and there was nothing in the apartment to eat that appealed to her. There was a Publix nearby in a strip shopping center that also had a drug store, a Thai restaurant, and a few other shops. She decided to do her grocery shopping and then get some Thai takeout. She hated to eat alone, especially at night, because she always felt like people were looking at her and wondering why she was by herself.

Once she arrived at the grocery store, she took out a long list of items she needed. She loaded her cart with all the basic spices and other supplies that you only had to buy occasionally, along with breakfast cereals, fruit, milk, chicken, a small package of steaks and the like. She was looking at the frozen dinners when she saw Jack Nebra, who was picking out some frozen yogurt for his cart. When he turned to place his choice in the cart, he saw her as well.

"Hello," he said smiling. "I saw you this morning at The Condor Company, but we were never introduced. I'm Jack Nebra."

"Yes. I recognized you from this morning. That was a little awkward, wasn't it? I'm Debra Raines, and today was to be my first day at work. I found out later that an employee had been killed. I guess that is why you were there?"

"Well, yes. How did you know that?"

"My father is a cop. Police Chief as a matter of fact, and a former FBI agent. I've been around law enforcement folks all my life. Call it an educated guess."

"I didn't realize I was that obvious. What do you mean this was to be your first day? Did something happen?"

"Well, the guy that was killed worked in the same section where I'll be working. It would not have really worked to introduce me at the same time they were telling the others about him, so the boss decided to just have me start Monday."

"Yeah, I can see where that would be a good idea. You must live around here?"

"I just moved into the Wind Song Townhouses, just down the street. That's why I'm here; I needed to stock up on some things."

"Well, we're neighbors, then. I live in the SunDown Apartments, just on the other side of you. I've been there about two years. This is a pretty good area."

The two talked easily together for another ten minutes, tentatively probing each other's background and current status, as young singles must do. Finally Debra looked at her watch.

"Jack, it has been really great talking to you, but I better get this stuff home and in the fridge."

Jack, having been given the second opportunity in the same day to meet this pretty and obviously intelligent girl, was not ready to give up so easily. "What are you doing for supper? Have you already eaten?"

"Well, I was just going to get some take out from the Thai restaurant over there."

"Their food is really good, but take out is pretty boring. I haven't eaten either, so why don't we just go over there and eat- in?"

"Well, I've got all this stuff that needs to go in the refrigerator..."

Jack looked at his cart that held several items that needed to be kept cool as well.

"Yeah, me, too. But we are only two blocks away. Why don't we check out, take our stuff back, and I'll pick you up in twenty minutes. Will that give you enough time?"

Debra hesitated and then decided, "Why not?" Jack was a good-looking man, and the first decent prospect to come her way in several months.

"Okay, that sounds good, but I'll just meet you back at the restaurant in about half an hour, okay?"

"Sure, if that suits you better. That sounds good. Thai sure beats the peanut butter and jelly sandwich I was planning on," he laughed.

Thirty minutes later they met at the restaurant. As they talked after ordering, both felt really good about the way the day was ending. They talked about a myriad of things.

Finally Debra said, "I've just got to ask you. What about the man that was killed? Do you have any idea who did it and why?"

"Now, being a cop's daughter and all, you know I can't tell you a whole lot. But, no, we haven't got a clue about who did it, or why. My gut feeling is that it wasn't just some random killing. But that might not be true, either. We just started working on it this morning. So, it's pretty soon to start jumping to conclusions."

"Dad always said the first seventy-two hours would generally tell the tale. He said if you didn't have a pretty good idea about who had committed the crime by then, that it got to be more and more difficult. Does that sound right to you?"

"Yes, that's about right. That doesn't mean we always solve a crime in seventy-two hours. Heck, sometimes we never solve them. But, you generally turn up most of the evidence within that time. I'll be glad to get the toxicology report from the coroner tomorrow. And, we have a few leads we need to chase down. I sure would like to catch whoever did it. Everything we've seen so far indicates the guy was a really good person."

"What do you expect the toxicology report to show?"

Jack shook his head and smiled. "Sorry, I really can't talk about that. Let's talk about something more fun. What are you doing Saturday?"

"I really don't have any plans."

"How would you like to go rafting on the Nantahala River? The weather is supposed to be great. The water will still be cold, but the outside temperature is expected to be in the eighties. We would have a great time."

"Well, that sounds like fun. I've heard about people doing that. How does it work?"

"Oh, there are a couple of ways to do it. You can go to one of the rafting companies that are on the river, and they will fix you up with a raft and life jacket and all, then they take a big group up river and everyone floats back down. They always send some guides with you. I've got a raft, so we could get another couple to go with us, leave one car down river and take the other up to where we want to put in. There are pros and cons to both ways. If you go with the group, they take care of everything, but you have to wait on them to get ready, and sometimes that's a pain, just standing around - but it's not that bad. The worst thing is they make you wear these funky life jackets. You can't bring your own. If we take my raft, we can pick and choose when to start and just do our own thing. But then, we have to hassle with two cars and making the trip back and forth up river. It's a pretty good drive up there. I've done it both ways, and they are both fun. So you tell me. Since you have never done it before, we'll do it whichever way you feel most comfortable."

"They both sound like fun. Since you are the expert, you choose."

"Well, why don't we do a combination? It's really pretty far to take two cars, if you are just going for the day, but it's also more fun if there are several people you know in your group. I'll call when I get home and see if this other couple I know can go. Then, I'll see if we can get reservations with one of the tour companies. If they've got room, we'll all just go with them, but if they don't we'll take my raft."

"That's fine. I'd like to meet your friends."

They talked for an hour longer - about the rafting trip, about each other, about fun things they had done. They were both open, honest, outgoing people, and the time flew by as they absorbed as much as they could about each other. By the time they parted, it was almost eleven, and Debra was very happy she had the next day off. Jack followed her home and winked his headlights at her as she turned into her drive.

-20-

The four men met in Wooten's office at two o'clock. None had eaten, and all were concerned about the day's events. As the men settled into their chairs, Wooten noted that Greg Bolin seemed the most agitated of the three.

Greg was the first to speak. "What is going on, J.P.? I didn't sign on for being an accessory to murder."

The others sat in stunned silence at the outburst. Wooten regarded Bolin coldly for a few moments.

"Greg, perhaps you would like to explain that statement. But before you do, let me remind you of something that you seem to have conveniently forgotten. Not only did you sign up for murder, you are directly responsible for several hundred deaths now, because of the balium that you introduced. Not me. Not Tim. Not Bill. You. You alone went to China. And you alone are responsible for the SARS epidemic. In fact, you could probably be classified as one of the world's worst mass murderers. So be very careful of making accusations that your have absolutely no evidence to make."

Greg's blood pressure must have skyrocketed. His face was red and the veins in his neck and temple protruded. He started to talk, and stopped himself. He visibly got control of his emotions and then spoke.

"I apologize. I did not mean that the way it came out. I am stressed about what's going on, and I spouted off when I should not have. But you are wrong about SARS, and you know it. We are all part of that, and we all know that once our cure is introduced, it will save lives. Yeah, I know people have died, and we can argue forever about whether they would have died anyway. What's got me upset is that now one of our staff has been killed. I worked with Gene everyday. He was one of us."

Wooten replied, "Look, Greg. He may have worked with you, but he was hardly your friend. Do I have to remind you that just two days ago, he tried to blackmail you and us? That you sent him home? That he was trying to take money out of all our pockets? Hey, I'm sorry the guy died, but it sure solves a problem for us, doesn't it?"

"So, you admit it? You had him killed?"

"I did not say that. Don't put words in my mouth. I said we are better off with him gone. That's all."

"I don't think we are better off if that detective finds out what's going on and ties it back to us. Did you know he asked us what balium was?"

This caused Wooten to sit back in his chair. "No, I didn't know that. What did he say, and what did you say to him? Why don't you and Tim tell us exactly what he asked, and what was said? Tim, you met with him first, right?"

"Yes. He was in Slaton's office when I got there with Ms. Raines. He wanted to meet with Greg because he was Windom's supervisor, so I volunteered to take him up. That way, Slaton could stay with Ms. Raines. Greg and I met with him in the conference room on the third floor."

Murray and Bolin related their entire conversation with Detective Nebra. At the end of the recitation, Wooten nodded and drummed his fingers on his desk.

"Well," he said, "That doesn't sound too bad. Just like you said, the 'balium equals SARS' could just mean that Windom was thinking that our research into the common cold might help us come up with a way to fight the illness. Nothing unusual about that. After all, he was a researcher for a pharmaceutical company. It would be odd if he wasn't thinking about how to cure something that is in the news everyday. I don't see a real problem, guys, do you?"

Greg spoke up. "I don't know. We don't know if that was the only thing Windom left behind, and we don't know what the detective might find. If someone who had broken in to rob him killed him, there will not be anything to lead him back to us. But if you had someone do it, then that means there is someone else out there that could lead back to you. And if you go down, I have no doubt, we will too. So, we've got a right to know. Did you have him killed?"

"No, I didn't. But maybe one of you did. After all, he was going to cost each of you a lot of money."

"I sure as hell didn't," said Murray, "and Greg obviously didn't. So what about it Bill, did you?"

Bill Horton looked as if he was the one who had been shot. "Of course not. I wouldn't do something like that. I would not even know how to go about contacting someone to do it."

"Well, that's that," said Wooten. "There's nothing to do now but wait. Let's move on. I think it's about time we make our move to introduce Cold-X. I have been re-thinking the best way to do it. I am not anxious to let other drug companies have time to analyze Cold-X, while we wait on our government, even if it is for only a short time. Rather than go to China, I was thinking about going to Washington next week and meeting with the folks at FDA. Maybe, see if I can get in to see the Surgeon General. Let them know we have the cure and try to come in the back door and get it approved in a hurry. I have some connections and some favors due, so it is worth a try. What do you think?"

Murray asked, "Do you think we ought to wait a little while, let this thing with Windom die down?

"I don't see why. We've got to do it sometime, or this whole thing was pointless. Once the word is out that we have a cure, the detective will just think that's what the note was about. Besides, even if I meet with them on Monday, it's not like they are going to make an announcement the next day. It will still take a while for them to agree to let us try the drug, and even longer before it is widely used. I think it will be the kind of thing where all of a sudden, here is this pill that seems to work, but is not approved. They'll use it on the most critical cases where they feel there is nothing to lose, because the patient is going to die anyway. They will keep using conventional, approved drugs on the others, until it becomes obvious that our drug works. By then, people will be so glad that a cure is available, they won't want to question it. It should all work out, just as we planned."

"I agree," said Murray. "Let's get on with it."

The others also agreed, and Wooten stood up, signaling the meeting's end.

"Okay, ya'll get out. I've got work to do."

They all left, feeling a sense of excitement. Only Greg Bolin's excitement was tempered. He was sure Wooten was lying about Windom, and he was not at all sure they had heard the last from Detective Nebra.

-21-

Mia Munson walked into the studio five minutes early. She still felt sleepy, but you could not tell it by looking. She was just a beautiful woman. Her flaming red hair and green eyes were striking, especially when she wore black, as she was now. Her makeup was immaculate, but would have to be touched up before she got under the TV lights.

She scanned the news lines that she was to read on the air. There was nothing new locally since this morning, except for a tanker truck jack-knifing on northbound I-85 almost at the juncture of I-75/85, which was about three miles from downtown Atlanta. Traffic had been tied up for hours. Other than that, it was the same old news. They just dressed it up differently. They would have a live report about yesterday's home invasion and killing that would basically recount what had happened and tell everyone to 'stay tuned for up to the minute updates, of which, there were none. On the national scene, there had been a car bombing on the Gaza Strip that killed seven, including one child; and there were two more deaths from SARS; one in Canada and one in China. Not a lot to report. But, by the time they did traffic and weather together every ten minutes and had the normal commercial breaks, it would take up the allotted hour.

She greeted her co-workers, and they exchanged pleasantries until time to go on the air. Several of them asked about Kent, which both pleased and depressed her. She shrugged off her thoughts of Kent as air-time approached and read over her script again.

Mia longed to do investigative reporting, but knew that she would never get the opportunity to do that in this job. Management had made it very clear that they wanted her on the air all of the time. She was aware that her looks played a large part in her getting this job, and they were also the reason the studio wanted her on camera. The station had trained her in speech and diction, and she knew that she carried herself well and presented a good on-camera presence. But, she also knew that she had a well functioning brain and could do far more than just read news bits that others had prepared for her. Her career was advancing rapidly, true enough, but she wanted more. She wanted the excitement of discovery and the satisfaction of actually obtaining the news, not just reading it.

"Time" was called, and she turned and smiled into the camera, and dutifully read the news.

-22-

Jack Nebra woke at seven and knew instantly what had bothered him about the office at Windom's house. That happened to him often. He would go to bed with something bothering him, or not clear, and when he woke up, he had the answer. It was like his mind rested, then went back to work while his body still slept. No longer bothered by outside influences, everything became clearer. It wasn't what was in the office; it was what wasn't there. There were no computer disks. He showered and dressed, ate a grapefruit for breakfast and headed to the office, coffee in hand. It was about a fifteen-minute drive in traffic, although it only took five minutes for the same drive when the roads were empty. Normally, Jack would listen to the news and talk on the phone while he drove. Today, he was almost at the office when he realized the radio was off. He had been thinking about Debra Raines. She seemed like a really great girl. Jack had felt so comfortable with her. He just felt in touch with her, as if they had been friends for a long time. She seemed too good to be true. He hoped not.

Once the newness of the relationship was over, he hoped there was still substance there.

When he got to the office, Detective Smith was already there. They met in Jack's office.

"Joel, do you remember seeing any computer discs at the house?" Jack asked before they even sat down.

"Uh, no. I don't," he answered.

"Well, how about checking that out first thing. Then, check with Dr. Chavez and see if those toxicology reports are back. I'm going to talk with Officer Newman," he said, looking at his notes. "He was the first one on the scene."

"What are you thinking, Jack?"

The two men talked for several minutes. They agreed to meet back in Jack's office after lunch, and Detective Smith left. Jack put in a call to the desk sergeant and asked that Officer Newman contact him as soon as possible. As luck would have it, it was the officer's day off, but they would contact him. Jack's desk held thick file folders on several other cases he was working on, and one he was going to have to testify about during the guy's trial next week. It was this folder he now selected.

Jack remembered the case well, but as he reviewed the file with his notes and pictures, it came vividly alive again. That was the way it should be for the trial, but Jack would rather have been able to forget all about it. The victim in the case was only ten months old. He had been shaken to death by his mother's live-in boyfriend, while the mother was away trying to score some drug money. The boyfriend had never had a real job and had been out of prison less than eighteen months. The mother, whose name was Latoya, had made her way through life having babies from a series of boyfriends, drawing welfare and living in public housing. She had her first baby when she was fifteen, and had successfully downloaded another just about each year after that. She was twenty-two, had five kids by five different men, no job and no life. It was a situation that was not uncommon, and it made Jack sick.

The children's grandmother kept the children normally, but she had gone to visit a sick sister in Vidalia, and Latoya was keeping the five children. Jerome Johnson, the boyfriend, was unable to quiet the crying baby, and in his frustration, had simply shaken the baby so hard that its tiny brain was fatally damaged. Little Jamal had never had much of a chance in life, given the conditions he was living in; now, he had none at all. The mother and boyfriend both claimed the baby had somehow fallen out of his crib. Dr. Chavez, the coroner, said differently.

Jack was a smart, tough detective, with a big heart. He loved children. He had a nephew the same age as the dead child, and it wrenched his heart to uncover the sordid details of the little one's brief existence. He did not know what to do about all the people living in public housing and having babies they could not support. But, he knew rewarding them with more money from the public trough was not the answer. A buddy of his had said that mothers on welfare should have to consent to sterilization, if they got pregnant while on the public dole, or the payments would stop. Jack used to think that was a pretty drastic measure. After seeing the squalor and deprivation these kids lived under, he had reconsidered. He knew that something needed to take place that would end the status quo. Kids having kids they can't afford and will not look after, just perpetuated the situation. They lived in filthy conditions, generally with just the mother and a series of boyfriends. Drugs were rampant, education scoffed at. It was a dead end life.

The ring from the phone on his desk interrupted his thoughts. It was Officer Newman.

"I appreciate your calling me back. I know it's your day off, so I won't keep you but a minute. I understand that you were the responding officer to the homicide yesterday?"

"Yes, we got the call and my partner, Sgt. Gailey, and I were there within ten minutes. We did not see any vehicles in the vicinity, so whoever did it, got out of there in a hurry. What's up?"

"Just trying to get a feel for the crime scene. Tell me what you did, and what you found."

"Well, when we got there the siren from the guy's alarm system was blaring loud enough to wake the neighbors. It was really loud. We knew that either no one was home, or there was a real problem. I checked the front door, and it was open. My partner called for back up, and we went ahead and went in. I know we should have waited, but that siren was driving us crazy, and I knew that no one had stuck around with that going off. Anyway, once we were inside, I turned left and found the guy in the bedroom. No one else was there. My partner found the alarm system in the closet and pulled off the wires that went to the siren. We secured the scene and called ya'll. That's about it."

"Were the lights on in the house?"

"No, all the lights were off."

"You are sure?"

"Sure, I'm sure. I had to use my flashlight. The drapes were pulled in the bedroom. and it was dark. Once I saw the body, I turned the lights on. of course, but they were off when we got there."

"Okay, thanks. That tells me what I needed to know. Have a good day, officer."

After hanging up, Jack got up, stretched and walked down the hall to get more coffee. The killer wouldn't have bothered to turn off the lights with that siren going, so that meant the lights were off the whole time. He could see the scene as it took place. The shooter was shining a bright light into the victim's eyes. He held the light in one hand and the pistol in the other, following Windom. He must have told him to get up. That is the only way the man would have gotten as far as he did. That also meant the killer wanted to talk to Windom or take him somewhere or show him something, because if he had just wanted him dead, he could have easily shot him while he was still in the bed. So, he had come for something - something he needed the victim's help to get. And, since Windom was dead beside the bed, he had not helped the killer at all. If what the killer wanted was in the house, it may still be there. He consulted his notes and got Windom's ex-wife's name and number. She agreed to meet with him, and Jack left for her house.

-23-

Debra Raines had slept well and woke refreshed. She put on her jogging outfit and went for a thirty minute run. She luckily found a side street where she could avoid car fumes. Her pace was strong and easy, and she covered a lot of ground. She enjoyed looking at the single family homes with their manicured lawns as she ran, trying to imagine what the people were like who lived there. Given the option, she would have chosen a country road, but this wasn't bad.

Once back at her apartment, she showered, dressed and had breakfast. She was glad for the unplanned day off, since she was going rafting on Saturday. Now, she would have time to pick up a few things for her apartment and do some other shopping. She decided that while she was out, she would go ahead and find the church that Mary Hightower had convinced her to attend Sunday. She had purchased a map of metro Atlanta and one of Douglas County. She got the latter one out now and located the church. It looked like it would be easy to get to, and it was not far from the mall where Macy's was located. Perfect.

She found the church easily, and decided to go in and get information about service times. She introduced herself to the secretary, saying she was one of Mary's friends and would visit on Sunday. The secretary, Kelly, took her on a tour of the church, which was a very modern facility with a great youth area and fellowship hall, as well as a library and a small prayer room. After the tour and picking up a church bulletin that gave not only the time of services, but also other information, Debra impulsively went back to the prayer room.

The room was only about six by six. There were two chairs, a small table and a cross. The light was soft and easily controlled by a dimmer switch on the wall. It had been a long time since Debra had been to church. Sitting now, with her head bowed, she prayed for the first time since her mother's funeral. She could feel a comfort washing over her that was both peaceful and exciting. She used to be a "regular" at church. Her parents were strong believers and had instilled that faith in their daughter. But when the tragedy occurred, it was as if she blamed God. She had heard many sermons about why bad things happen to good people, but that had not mattered. Her mother was dead and her family broken; someone needed to pay for that, and that would be God. She punished Him by not going to church or acknowledging Him. As she sat there, tears running down her cheeks, Debra knew that a self-imposed isolation was over. God still loved her, and she felt cleansed.

When she drove away from the church, Debra did not know whether it would become her church home. But she knew some church soon would be.

Her thoughts turned to Jack Nebra, as she drove. He seemed like such a great guy. He was clean cut, articulate and handsome. She had enjoyed his company, and was looking forward to being with him on Saturday. It would be fun, and she would get to watch him interact with his friends. She had learned that you could tell a lot about someone when you see how people they know well treat them. It should be an interesting and exciting day.

One of the items Debra needed to pick up was a bathing suit for tomorrow. She figured they would probably wear shorts and tops over bathing suits, but she still wanted a new one. She selected two that were more modest than the others, which was not saying much, she thought. When they both fit perfectly, she decided to splurge and bought them both. She spent another hour and a half shopping, then ate lunch in the food court and went home.

She returned to her apartment and saw that she had a message. "Hey sweetheart, this is Dad. I was thinking about you and missing you. I'd like to come see you when it's convenient and try to make up for some lost time. I'm sorry I missed you. Give me a call when you can." There was a pause in the message, then, "I love you, Deb, and I'm sorry I haven't been a very good Dad, lately. I hope you'll forgive me."

For the second time that day, she cried.

-24-

Jim Wooten arrived at his office early on Friday. He looked up George Champion's telephone number on his palm pilot.

George Champion was the President's Assistant Chief of Staff, and a friend of Wooten's. As good a friend as a hundred thousand dollars in contributions can buy. He returned the call before Wooten had finished the donut and coffee he was having for breakfast.

"Jim! How are you? I haven't talked to you in a while. How is everything?"

"Hello, George. I'm fine. How is the family?"

The men made small talk for a minute. Then George asked, "What can I do for you, Jim?"

"Well, I would like to come to Washington as soon as possible next week, and I need to get in to see some people. It's important."

"What's it about, and who do you want to see?"

"George, my company has developed a cure for SARS. We have been working on a drug for the common cold for quite some time, and we have found that it cures SARS. I know I need to see Joan Hadley over at the FDA, and probably the Surgeon General, Dr. Conner. I don't really know who else. I was hoping you might be able to guide me there. We know the process that we normally go through, but with this epidemic, we need to fast track it, and that's something we need help doing. We have tested it, and this stuff absolutely works."

"Jim, are you serious? That is fantastic! You are sure about this?"

"You'd better believe, I'm serious. When they see this medicine work, they are going to be so excited, they'll probably pee all over themselves."

George laughed. "I'd pay to see that. Let me call you back in a couple of hours, Jim. Is this the best number to get you?"

Jim confirmed that it was, and they hung up. He finished his donut and stood at the window, enjoying the view and smoking his cigar. Things were moving along nicely, he thought. Bolin was the only one he had to worry about. He was smart and outspoken, but he tended to jump before he thought things all the way through. That could be dangerous. Like this thing with Windom. Here Bolin was all holier-than-thou about that killing, when there were so many more that had died from SARS. That detective had really scared him, coming with no warning and all. Heck, he scared me, too, Wooten admitted to himself.

George Champion called back about two hours later. Condor had an impeccable reputation, and no one took Wooten's claim lightly. Wooten had a meeting at two in the afternoon on

Monday with the Surgeon General and Joan Hadley, as well as a few other interested personnel. If everything was the way Wooten had described it, The Condor Corporation was going to be getting a lot of exposure. Wooten hung up the phone and smiled. This called for a celebration. He called one of his current honeys, who was very excited about an evening on the town. He told his secretary to call the charter service and book a plane for him and reservations at the Watergate for two nights. Then, he left for his usual Friday golf game.

-25-

J ack Nebra and Detective Smith met back at headquarters after lunch, and compared notes. Jack had struck out with Windom's ex-wife. She could not imagine why anyone would want to hurt Gene. He had not been acting strange, had not told her anything that seemed out of ordinary. He had been a great father and had never missed a child support payment. Normally, cops always looked at close kin, especially an ex-spouse, as a prime suspect. This woman was so open, so obviously honest and so distraught that Jack pretty much eliminated that possibility. Remembering the bottle of Scotch, he had asked her about Windom's drinking habits. She had told him that it was not often and not much when he drank. The one thing that she did confirm was that Gene kept a box of floppy discs right beside the computer.

Detective Smith had gone back by the house and confirmed there were no computer disks in the office or in any drawers in the house. He had also checked with the Coroner's office and gotten the toxicology report. Windom had a high blood alcohol level. Considering the fact that he had probably been asleep for several hours, he was probably legally drunk at the time he went to bed.

Jack told Smith of his conversation with the responding officer.

"What do you make of it, Jack?"

"I'm thinking the killer came to the house looking for something. I'm thinking he took the computer discs, hoping what he was looking for was on them. But, he wasn't sure he had what he came for, because he was making Windom get out of bed. The only reason he would do that was so he could get Windom to show or give him something. Windom was probably sleeping so soundly the perp had time to take a good look around before he woke him.

"Or, maybe he was going to take Windom with him," said Smith.

Nebra considered this. "Maybe. But if it were me, and someone were pointing a gun at me and wanted me to come with them, I'd be tempted to go along and wait for a better opportunity to overtake him. Windom had to know the chances of him setting off the alarm, getting the gun, and shooting someone who was already pointing a gun at him and blinding him with light was pretty slim. So slim that he would have taken that chance only if he thought he was going to die anyway. I think that he was in something way over his head. He had information that this guy wanted badly enough to kill for, and it was information that could conceivably be on a computer disc."

"Well, he was a research scientist for Condor. Do you think he had information about something he was working on that someone either wanted or, at least, did not want him to have?"

"Yes, that's the only thing that has come to mind. I think we need to know more about what he was working on, and more about the people he was working with." He thought a minute. "Go ahead and do a quick check on the people I talked with the other day. I don't think you'll find anything, but I want to be sure. We need to know the names of the other people in his department, and run some checks on them as well." He handed Bolin, Slaton and Murray's business cards to Smith. "Make copies of these, they are the guys I met with. Bolin was Windom's supervisor; he'll probably give you the information over the phone about the others on Windom's team."

Smith left and Nebra spent the rest of the day reviewing other case files and catching up on paperwork. About five he called his friend, Mike, and invited him and Jen to go rafting the next day. Mike was excited about the idea, and they decided to leave around nine. Jack was able to make reservations at a whitewater rafting company he was familiar with, so they would be able to ride up together. With that decided, Jack called Debra.

"Are you just now waking up?" he kidded when she answered the phone.

"No," she laughed, "But I did sleep late. I was out past my bedtime! But I have accomplished a lot today. How about you? Have you made any progress finding your killer?"

"Not as much as I would have liked, but we've made a little headway. Tied up a few loose ends and all. Hey, I talked with my friend, Mike. He and his wife, Jen, are on to go with us tomorrow. We plan to leave about nine. Will that work for you?"

"That sounds great. What do I need to bring?"

"Your bathing suit and some shorts and top you don't mind getting wet, a towel and a change of clothes for the trip home. There are some showers and dressing rooms up there. They aren't the greatest, but at least it's something. That's it. We'll pick up something for lunch on the way."

"Okay, I can do that. I'll be ready by nine. What time do you think we'll get back? "

"Before dark, probably around seven. Hey, we can pick up some steaks and grill them down by the pool at my place. They have a little area there called 'The Gathering Spot' with four or five outside grills and a little clubhouse where you can get a sandwich or drinks and play games. It's pretty fun."

Debra agreed, and they each reluctantly hung up the phone. Jack had started to ask her what she was doing tonight, but thought that might be moving a little fast. He decided to go over to another friend's house and help him build the Austin Healy 3000 kit car he had been working on for over a year. He called his buddy, who was also single and definitely intended to stay that way. They decided to meet for supper at Vick's Barbeque House, then go to the garage and work on the car.

-26-

G reg Bolin left early on Friday. He and Sally, a short, buxom blonde he had taken out several times, were going to spend the weekend on his houseboat at Lake Lanier, and he needed to pick up some supplies. He stopped at the liquor store and grocery store, and then he picked up Sally, who had a small, neat home just west of Douglasville. He hoped to beat the worst of the downtown traffic, which was always bad in the early morning and afternoon, but was especially horrendous on Fridays. It was only about forty-five miles to the lake, but you had to travel through downtown on I-85 or take I-285, which circled the outskirts of Atlanta, and then get on I-85 on the north side. Sally was waiting for him, and they got a good start.

It was only four o'clock, so Greg decided to chance I-85. He took I-20 out of Douglasville, which crosses over both of these interstates, and Greg noticed that I-285 was running smoothly, when they crossed over it. They knew they were in trouble as soon as they took the exit to 75/85 North. Traffic was bumper to bumper, both North and South bound, and stop and go. He had forgotten about the Braves game. Fortunately, the traffic opened up somewhat after the 75-85 split, and they were able to pick up their speed. The Jaguar purred powerfully, and Greg opened the moon roof. This helped his attitude tremendously, much to Sally's gratitude. She had never seen Greg so uptight, and had been regretting her decision to spend the weekend with him. He had cursed and pounded the steering wheel and constantly moved from one lane to another he thought might be moving faster. Nothing worked, and it had taken them over an hour to travel ten miles. There had been no conversation between them to speak of during that time, and the tension on Greg's face was visible.

"I'm sorry," he said now. "I've had a rough week at work, and that traffic just capped it off." He offered her a half-smile, and Sally patted his hand.

"Tell me about it. Maybe it will make you feel better."

"Actually, I would rather just forget about it. Things have been really hectic getting our drug Cold-X ready. It looks like it may be the cure for SARS. Wooten is going to Washington next week to see about putting it on the fast track so they can use it. And then yesterday, I get to work and find out that Gene Windom, who was my top research assistant on the project, had been killed when someone broke into his home."

"Oh, no. I saw that on the news, but I didn't realize he worked for you. I'm sorry. But that's great about the SARS drug. I hope that works out."

"Yeah. Hey, it's going to be a beautiful weekend. We'll get to the boat just in time to have a few drinks and grill some trout.

We'll just stay in the slip tonight and then move on to another area tomorrow. I'm going to forget about all that and try to be a better companion."

Sally smiled, feeling better and better about the weekend now that Greg seemed more like himself.

♦♦♦

Bill Horton had arrived at his Inman park home about five and immediately fixed a double scotch, as was his custom. He turned on the television to watch the six o'clock news and looked through his mail, and the front page of The Atlanta Journal. The murder of Gene Windom had been front-page news yesterday. Now, he could not find anything about it. Mia Munson of NewsNow briefly mentioned it, and that was it. It was yesterday's news and soon forgotten. And that was fine with him.

Horton had not said anything in the meeting in Wooten's office, primarily because the whole thing dumbfounded him. But, he had thought of it a lot since then, and he thought Bolin might be right. If that detective got the idea that Windom's killing was somehow connected to Condor, this whole thing could explode. The last thing they needed was someone snooping around. Until now the only thing connecting them to SARS was that paper they all stupidly signed. But the investigation of Windom's death made everything more risky.

He was glad that Wooten was going to Washington and getting things going. It was time. They needed some big money to cover his illegal books, and they needed it now. He was nervous about the books. He was scared about the detective looking into Windom's death. He needed another drink.

After a few drinks, he felt better and decided to walk to the diner at the end of the block to get supper. He was a regular there, and the waitresses knew him by name. He ignored the homeless man sitting on the corner with his "homeless, please help" sign and entered the diner. He sat alone, as always, and finished reading the paper he had brought with him. He liked it here because he fit right in. Most of the people were there by themselves, so he did not feel strange eating alone. There were rarely any couples, just a few construction workers or area clerks, and every now and then a vagrant who had decided to eat his meal rather than drink it. Horton, with his frumpy clothes and disheveled appearance, felt comfortable here. He was a lonely man, in a lonely place.

♦♦♦

Tim Murray and his wife, Ellen, went to the Bear's Paw Brewery for supper. The restaurant was only about ten minutes from their house, had great food and a good selection of beer brewed in the huge stainless steel vats that were part of the restaurant's décor. They waited about thirty minutes for a table, even though it was only six o'clock when they arrived. Although Ellen knew of Windom's death and that Condor had a cure for SARS, neither event was very important to her. Tim did not like to talk about things that happened at work, and that was fine. She did not want to know.

Now she talked about her tennis match, her volunteer work and the weather. Tim pretty much zoned her out, listening just enough to nod his head from time to time. His thoughts were entirely on Windom and Cold-X. Wooten's optimism had encouraged him, but there was a niggling doubt that troubled him. If Bolin was right and the detective did connect the murder to Condor, it could mean the end of everything. He looked at his wife and wondered what she would say if she knew the truth. Probably not much, as long as they didn't get caught, and it did not affect her lifestyle, he concluded.

But his children were a different matter. Tim had accomplished a lot in life, but it was his children who made him the proudest. They were both wonderful kids. Smart, good-looking and popular, they meant more to him than anyone or anything. Dad was their hero and they would be devastated to find out he was involved in anything that was remotely illegal. That just could not happen, he thought now. He had worked too hard to create this wonderful life they all enjoyed. He had gotten into this in order to protect that lifestyle. He was used to being in control of situations. Now there was a detective out there looking into a murder that could bring the whole company down, and he could not do anything about it. Wooten had made the decision to have Windom killed, Murray was sure, and he had not consulted the others. Horton was a slob and he didn't trust him. Bolin was smart, but he was also prone to leap before he looked. And Tim was dependent on each one. He was not in control, and he was very nervous about that.

The food was delicious. It just didn't taste very good to him.

-27-

Saturday was one of those days of promise that actually lived up to expectations. The sun was bright in a cloudless sky, and there was just enough breeze for comfort. Early morning temperatures in the low seventies would climb to eighty-two in the afternoon. Jack had picked Debra up right at nine o'clock. Then they went back to pick up Mike and Jen. After introductions, the foursome left for their rafting excursion, excited about their adventure and the prospect of getting to know each other better. Traffic was very light, and they were able to make good time.

The scenery was beautiful as they passed through the Georgia Mountains and made their way over to South Carolina. Conversation between the four was easy and fun. Mike was a teacher, and he kept them all laughing with his stories of his student's antics. Jen was a freelance writer and was working on a story about the kaolin mines in middle Georgia where "Georgia white dirt" is mined. Jack and Debra were surprised to learn that some people ate the dirt, which is actually clay. Jen told them that it is used medically in products like Maalox and Rolaids. Those that ate it swore by its medicinal value. Mike and Jen wanted to know more about the murder that Jack was investigating, especially when they found that Debra would be working for the same company and in the same area as the victim, but Jack was reluctant to talk about an on-going investigation. Instead, he told them about little Jamal and the case he would testify about in court the following week. This led to a lively discussion about the culture that fostered such tragic events and the pros and cons of sterilization and welfare. The group was having fun, and the three-hour ride was quickly over.

They decided to eat lunch in the small town of Demarest, which was near the Whitewater Rafting Adventure company where they had reservations. They were early for their one o'clock check in time, so decided to eat at a trendy looking café, rather than just get fast food. They found a table in the shade with a wonderful view of the Great Smoky Mountains. Mike soon had them in stitches telling them about one of his students who constantly talked about his momma's best friend, Theresa, who obviously had a weight problem.

"If Theresa was here, wouldn't be no food for nobody. Woman would eat the hide right off a live cow," he mimicked his student.

They finished their meal and drove up the mountain road into the Nantahala National Forest, where the river is located. They passed several different companies offering whitewater-rafting experiences before they arrived at the one which was their destination. They checked in and about twenty minutes later everyone was called for an orientation meeting where they were told some of the basics, like how to hold the paddle and what to do if, or rather, when, someone fell into the river, which was a chilly sixty-four degrees. Once this was done, they selected life jackets, which were every bit as funky as Jack had said they would be, and loaded onto an old school bus for the drive up the mountain. Thankfully, every window on the bus was wide open, because all forty passengers were wearing sour smelling life vests. Debra was glad to know showers were available, because she knew they would all need one.

The Nantahala River is crystal clear and shallow. There would be about seven rafts in their group and three guides. One guide would be in the boat with them. He explained they would be experiencing some class I and II rapids, and a class III rapid at the end of the trip, which would be about eight miles long and take about three hours. Debra and Jack sat opposite each other in the front of the raft. They sat on the side of the raft in the manner they were instructed and shoved their feet under the edge to help hold them in. Mike sat in the middle behind Debra, and Jen behind Jack to balance the raft. The guide sat in the rear center. Once loaded, they started out and were followed by the other rafts in the group.

Debra had never been rafting, and she was amazed at how peaceful and tranquil it was. They could see other rafts in front of theirs and could tell by the way those rafts were bouncing the trip was soon to be more exciting. Still, Debra was totally unprepared for the ice-cold water that hit her in the face as they bounced down the first rapids. She was quickly drenched from head to toe. She would not have been wetter if she had fallen in. She laughed and used her paddle to splash Jack with water. Before long the whole group was wet and laughing, and the guide was not sure he was on the right raft. Everyone had a wonderful time, and Debra endeared herself to the other three with her laughter and obvious athleticism.

They managed to finish the trip without actually falling in the water, although none of the other rafters would have believed that from their appearance. They showered and changed and thus, refreshed, headed for home.

Jen and Mike had said yes when asked if they wanted to join them at The Gathering Spot to grill steaks, so while Jack and Mike burned the meat, Jen and Debra fixed salad and desert at Jen and Mike's apartment. The four ate supper there and then played Scattergories. It was almost midnight when Jack took Debra back to her place.

"Well, you win the prize, Jack."

"Prize?"

"Yes. That is not only the longest date I have ever had, it was the most fun. Thank you for including me. It was all great. Jen and Mike are a really nice couple, and I enjoyed meeting them, too."

"Yeah, they are super. We'll get together with them again, if you would like. That is if you'll go out with me again," he smiled.

"I'd love to."

For the first time since they met each other, there was some awkwardness, as neither knew the best way to say good night. Finally, Jack held both of her hands and kissed her on the forehead. "Goodnight, Debra, I had a great time, too. I hope you sleep well. I'll call you soon."

"Please do."

Jack waved, as he walked back to his car. And Debra went inside her apartment where she leaned with her back against the door. She was exhausted, and excited about this new relationship. Jack seemed like a rare man, and she was more than a little attracted to him. She decided she was too keyed up to sleep, so she poured a glass of wine and turned on the news. Mia Munson, looking even prettier than Debra remembered, was finishing the NewsNow eleven o'clock show and was telling the viewers goodnight.

Debra wondered if Mia and Kent were still together. She had never blamed Mia for hers and Kent's breakup. She had known all along that she had pretty much driven Kent away. Sure, for a while she had resented the idea that he jumped into that relationship so quickly, but she had gotten over that long ago. And, looking at Mia now, she could not blame him. Filled with euphoria about her blooming relationship with Jack, she tilted her wine glass toward the television and wished Mia and Kent well. Then she went to bed.

-28-

Jim Wooten left his home about nine on Monday and drove to Tara Field, a small airport located on Tara Boulevard about ten minutes south of his home. The airport, which is in Henry County, is actually owned by Clayton County and Jim smiled again about the politics of that situation. He parked at Smith Air and ten minutes later he was seated comfortably in one of their Lear Jets and waiting for take-off. This is the way to do it, he thought. No lines. No parking fees. No security checks. Just drive up, get on the plane and leave. He would be in Washington in just over an hour, plenty of time to check in at the Watergate Hotel and get some lunch before his meeting. He had samples of Cold-X with him, as well as copies of research papers and tests. He was confident his mission would be successful and he was excited to finally be getting started with it.

He had talked with George Champion Friday evening, and George had promised to have a limo waiting for him at Reagan field. Wooten had long been a heavy contributor to both the

Democrats and the Republicans, because he wanted to have friends in high places, regardless of who was in power. He knew, and just as importantly, George knew, that if Cold-X was fast tracked and allowed on the market, his donation to the Democratic Party would increase substantially. Wooten smiled. He loved politics and money and the power of each.

The plane ride was short, smooth and eventless, just like he liked them. The pilot had called ahead, and the limo was waiting for him when he exited the plane. The chauffeur handed Wooten an envelope and they got in and headed for the hotel. Wooten opened the letter from Champion, which told him he would meet him in the lobby of the Watergate at one o'clock. Wooten checked in, ordered a sandwich from room service, and freshened up. When the sandwich came, he ate while reviewing his file and presentation. He exited the elevator into the lobby at precisely one o'clock and walked over to George Champion.

The men greeted each other warmly as they shook hands.

"Jim, there are a lot of people excited about this. A whole lot of people. You and your company's reputation are well known, so we know you aren't just blowing smoke. I hope you have everything you need, 'cause there's a room full of powerful folks wanting to see what you have."

"Well, I think I've got what I need, so let's don't keep them waiting. I don't want them all looking at their watches when we walk in."

"Okay, I'm parked right outside. We are meeting at the Pentagon, so it'll just take us a few minutes to get there. I'll

Fatal Healing

give you a run down of who all's there as we ride." They got into a black Mercedes at curbside and George continued. "Okay, besides Joan Hadley of the EPA and Surgeon General Conner, my boss, Lynn Means, whom I think you know, will be there. Then George Folsom, who represents the Secretary of State, will be there, as well as Jim Grissom, who heads up our foreign relations. There will probably be some aides of other interested parties there as well. The conference room we will use holds about twenty-five, and I imagine it will be full. Like I said, you have generated a lot of excitement."

"Alright. That sounds good. I'm anxious to show ya'll what I have."

The guard at the gate passed them through, and they entered the building where a visitors' pass was waiting for Jim Wooten. George led the way over to the elevator, and they rode to the second floor, and to a conference room where there was lively conversation until they entered.

"Everyone, this is Jim Wooten, president of The Condor Corporation. Jim, let me introduce you to these folks."

He went around the room and introduced Jim to each person, who also wore a security badge with his or her name on it. After the introductions, he pointed to the podium at the front of the room.

"There's a built in microphone, and the overhead projector you wanted. Do you need anything else, or can I help with the overhead?"

"No, I think I've got it," Wooten said, and walked to the front. He withdrew a thin folder from his brief case and placed the first paper in the overhead. He was polished and confidant, and even the most doubtful in the audience were impressed with his bearing.

"Ladies and gentlemen, thank you for coming today. I promise that you will be glad you did. George already told you who I am. Let me take about two minutes to tell you about Condor as a lead in to the main reason we are all here. Condor is a well-established pharmaceutical company with annual sales exceeding one billion dollars. We have a top-notch research team with more than three hundred employees, including over one hundred scientists and staff. We have a number of successful drugs on the market that have helped countless people across the world. About five years ago we started in earnest trying to find a cure for the common cold. We put our best people on the project and spared no expense in the research. I'm sure that all of the other pharmaceutical companies out there are looking for the same thing. But we have been fortunate enough to find it. In fact, our test results and data and application for FDA approval have been prepared, and I have a copy of that with me."

I am sure that you know that SARS, for lack of a better word, is a glorified cold. It is meaner, more contagious, and more devastating, but the specific characteristics are the same."

He turned on the overhead and a chart listing the symptoms and conditions and intensities of SARS and a cold was projected on screen. The common cold and SARS were identical, except for the intensities of the symptoms.

"We have tested our drug and are 100% successful in treating the common cold."

When Wooten said this, there were significant looks between some of those in attendance, and just about everyone leaned forward in their chair. The 100% success rate had captured them. He presented several overhead charts that backed up his words.

He continued. "We obtained strains of the SARS virus for our research. He paused for effect. We were 100% successful, and I have the results here for you to look at. I brought about fifteen copies of these test results with me, but we'll get more made so you can each have a copy. I'm sure you know that I would not be standing before you today and making these claims, if I could not back them up. The problem is that it would normally take at least two years to get FDA approval for the drug, and at the rate SARS is moving, that will mean many thousands of deaths and whole economies ruined. What I am proposing is that we take Cold-X and put it to the ultimate 'field test,' if you will. We will provide the drug at our cost to China and Canada, and they can use it to treat only those who have no other hope. Once the results are in, then the demand will be there for treating everyone with it, and I would want immediate FDA approval."

Joan Hadley, spoke up. "Nothing is keeping you from just providing those test results and the drug to China now. Your company is well known and they would certainly try the drug. Why do you need us?"

Wooten smiled. "Ms. Hadley, I appreciate your question and your compliment. But we are an American company, and, while I may dislike the approval process that we must go through here to get our drugs approved, it is that very process and the stamp of approval that not only the people in the United States have come to rely on, but people around the world. You are right, I could probably have the drug in use in short order, but health care professionals everywhere would still have reservations without the FDA stamp. Further, we would still not have the drug approved for use in the United States, and our competitors over here would have access to our product and have a two-year head start in being able to introduce their own version. We've spent many millions on this research, and I'm not inclined to give the competition that opportunity to catch us. If we introduce the drug, it needs to be with preliminary approval from FDA, and assurances that once proven in the field, final approval will be forth coming without delay."

"But, as you said, it is the very process that gives us credibility that you are wanting us to by-pass."

"I don't want to by-pass the testing. FDA will have ample opportunity to observe the drug being used on a wide variety of humans. In fact, many more than you would see in any control group. It is all the paperwork and endless documentation and feasibility studies that I am wanting to by-pass. You will have every opportunity to observe the reactions to the drug. If it doesn't work, if there are too many adverse reactions, then I would expect you to withhold your approval. But I am confident that Cold-X will work, and work well."

The meeting went on for several hours. Wooten was pleased with the overall tone of the meeting as those in attendance started questioning how the approval and introduction and announcements about the drug should take place, rather than if they should take place.

Finally Lynn Means, White House Chief of Staff spoke up. "Mr. Wooten, I think that it would be best if we had the opportunity to discuss this among ourselves. I am grateful to you for coming today, and I am excited about the possibilities. Will you stay in town at least through tomorrow in case we need to meet again? I know the President is most anxious to hear about how we progress today."

"Yes, I will be in Washington through tomorrow. Longer, if you need me to be. Here is my card with my cell number. You can reach me 24/7 on that."

He stood to gather his things and George Champion helped him. They shook hands all around and left the others to discuss the fate of Cold-X.

"Jim, that went well. It was a good presentation. I think Ms. Hadley just has to reach a comfort level with it. Like you said, she'll have the biggest test group ever. I'll also tell you, there are some real political advantages if the United States steps up and has a cure and offers it unconditionally. There are a lot of people around the world who think we are overbearing and only out for ourselves, even though we give far more than any other country to fight world hunger and suffering. It's incredible. They just point out how rich our country is, like that is a sin or something. Anyway, SARS is in the headlines everyday the world over. We could not buy the kind of press we would get if we provided the cure. That wouldn't hurt your company either!" He laughed as he slapped Wooten on the back.

The Mercedes pulled back in front of the Watergate Hotel. "What are your plans for the rest of the day, Jim?"

"Oh, I've got some paperwork to catch up on. If I finish that, I may wander around a little. I haven't been here in a couple of years."

"How about supper? Unless you already have plans, I'll plan on picking you up around seven."

"Alright George. But don't feel like you need to baby-sit me. If you have something else to do, I'll be fine."

"I'm looking forward to it. See you at seven."

As Champion drove off, Wooten thought wryly to himself that this would prove to be a very expensive meal. George Champion would surely hit him up for a big contribution tonight. After all, the President had some stiff competition for the upcoming election.

-29-

Detectives Nebra and Smith met in Jack's office at eleven o'clock on Monday morning.

"What have you got on the background checks, Joel?"

"Well, there is nothing more than a traffic ticket on anybody but Slaton."

Jack looked up from his notepad. "And what's the story on him?"

"He had a few charges against him for unnecessary roughness, when he was a cop, but they were later dropped. Apparently, the last one was pretty bad. It looks like they were dropped in exchange for his resignation. He had been with Atlanta P.D. for a long time and seemed to have good reports other than that. You will love this. He won a few metals for sharp shooting."

"Is that right? Interesting. What about prior to being on the force, anything there?"

"Military. He served three tours in Nam. He was never wounded, but obviously loved combat. Received a whole passel of medals. Apparently that is where he learned to shoot. He even represented the Army on the pistol team. He won a few competitions down at Fort Benning."

"Why did he get out?"

"Don't know. Just shows he was honorably discharged, lists his stations and medals. He started with Atlanta P.D. right after discharge. It was just after we pulled out of Vietnam; a lot of people left at that time. Nothing unusual there."

"Let's dig a little deeper on him. See if you can get more information about him from the Army. I know there are a lot of people that can shoot a pistol well, but the pattern in Windom's chest is the tightest I've seen."

"You think he did it?"

"I just think we need to consider that possibility. Right now, he is the only choice we have. Did you have any luck with Windom's neighbors?"

"No. They knew him well enough to wave at him when he drove past and speak to him at the mailbox. One of the neighbors had a little girl about the same age as his children, and they would play together some. Harris is their name. The mother said Windom kept pretty much to himself, except when the kids were around. Then he would play with them and take them skating and stuff. But no one had seen anyone else with him and nothing suspicious. That is a dead end. Nothing there."

"What about the folks he worked with directly; have you checked them out?"

"Not yet. Bolin left early Friday. I'll give him a call in just a little bit."

"Why don't we grab some lunch and just go back out there. I want to see Slaton again."

The two men discussed a few other aspects of the case and then left for lunch. Smith drove as Jack looked over his notes. He always found it helpful to go back to the beginning as cases progressed, to see if earlier notes made more sense in light of new evidence. The men arrived at the Condor Corporation just after one o'clock. The gate guard recognized Jack from the first visit.

"We need to see Rex Slaton," Jack told the guard.

The guard looked a little confused. "Was he expecting you? 'Cause if he was, he screwed up. He told us his son was out of school today, and they went on a fishing and camping trip on Sunday and were coming back later today. He said he had a new boat they needed to try out."

Jack considered this. "No, I did not have an appointment. How about Greg Bolin? Is he here?"

"Let me call him."

A few minutes later they were allowed through the gate and parked in the visitors area. Bolin met them at the front desk and got them visitor's badges. Jack introduced him to Detective Smith.

"I'm sorry to barge in on you like this. We actually came to see Rex Slaton, but he isn't here. We really just had a couple of questions for you. Is there a place we can talk a few minutes?"

Greg Bolin took them back to the third floor conference room, talking to them about their weekend along the way. Jack mentioned the rafting trip, but not Debra Raines.

Bolin closed the conference room door. "How can I help you detective?"

"We just need to get a list of people that Mr. Windom was working with. We are going to need to talk with them individually. You will be welcome to sit in if you like."

"You want to talk to them today?"

"Well, we had not really planned to do it today; we just wanted to get a list of who they are. But if it works better for you, we can do it now. It probably won't take more than five minutes each. We just want to ask them a few questions. They worked with him everyday. We just need to know if they noticed anything suspicious."

Greg thought for a moment. "Well, I don't guess it matters which day you do it. Let me call Tim Murray, since he is VP of Personnel, and just let him know. He may want to sit in, too."

Murray answered Greg's call and came down to the conference room. He talked with the detectives while Bolin went to get the first of Windom's co-workers. True to Jack's word, the questions were short and the interviews with them took less than two hours. No one had noticed anything unusual. Two said that Windom had seemed a little uptight about something, but neither had any idea what it was.

Nebra had the names and needed information on each of the co-workers and would continue to check them out. From all appearances it would be a wasted effort. All had been open and anxious to help.

The two detectives left and Bolin and Murray went back to their respective offices, certain they had dodged another bullet.

Jack and Detective Smith left in Smith's car. "Joel, while you are looking into Slaton's military background, go ahead and check him out further. Where does he live? How much money do he and his wife make? What are their expenses? How many kids in school? You know. I want to know everything about him that we can learn without a court order. And find out when and where he got that new boat, and how he paid for it."

Nebra remembered one more thing and took out Greg Bolin's business card. "Mr. Bolin, this is Detective Nebra. There was one more thing that I wanted to ask you about. Was there a SARS conference in Hong Kong?"

Greg Bolin was glad he was sitting at his desk and that Nebra was not looking at him, because perspiration had immediately covered his brow. "Not that I'm aware of," he was able to say.

"Well, is one planned that you know about?"

"No, why?"

"Well, it was on that paper that Windom had been doodling on. It said, "balium=s SARS Conference =s Hong Kong." Does that mean anything to you?"

"No, I'm sorry it doesn't"

"Okay. Thanks. If something comes to mind, give me a call."

The men hung up the phone and Nebra stared out the window. He was pretty sure Bolin was lying to him, and he wondered about that for quite a while.

Greg Bolin hung up and just sat at his desk, head in hand, and he wondered too. He wondered what else was in Windom's house or on that paper, and what other surprises from Detective Nebra were coming.

-30-

Debra Raines arrived at work early on Monday and used her new security card and retina scan to enter the research area of the building. She found her way to Mary Hightower's desk. She sat, leafing through a magazine until the secretary arrived.

"Good Morning, Debra! You are here early this morning. Are you that anxious to start work?"

Debra laughed. "I guess I am! I'm a little apprehensive, but I'm definitely ready to get started."

"Well, let's give it about thirty minutes and let everyone get here. Then, I'll take you around and introduce you, and you can get an idea of where you want to work. I want to tell you again that I was thrilled to see you at church yesterday. I didn't know if you would remember. How did you like it?"

"It's a great church. Everyone was very friendly, especially when I told them you had invited me! And the preacher was good, too. It was like he was just talking to us, and I like that.

I'm not very fond of those preachers that think yelling and modulating their voice is the way to preach."

"He is a fine preacher. I hope you will visit us again soon."

The two talked for several more minutes, and Debra told her about the rafting trip. She felt a little like she used to when she would tell her mother about her dates and fun things they had done, and it felt good.

"That sounds so wonderful, Debra! What a great way to spend the day. I'm glad that you have already found some friends here. What do they do for a living?"

"Mike is a school teacher; Jen is a free-lance writer; and Jack is a detective." Debra did not tell Mary that Jack was investigating the murder of Mr. Windom, because she just did not want to bring up that subject.

"Wow, it sounds like they all have interesting jobs. I'll bet they are fun people."

They talked for several more minutes, and Mary walked with Debra to the break room to get coffee. They met several other employees there and Mary introduced them. Everyone was friendly and seemed genuinely glad to have her there. They finished their coffee, and Mary took her around to meet the others.

It took over two hours to make the rounds of the various research groups, and that was just getting a whirlwind tour. There were ten teams working on over twenty projects. Each team worked on at least two at a time, because sometimes there were delays due to testing, or waiting for results of tests, and that way everyone could stay busy. Most, but not all the time, the teams would have projects that were on opposite ends of the development cycle. They might have one that research was just beginning on and another where it was winding down. There were a few teams with three projects, and generally the third was one that had been around for ages, according to Mary. Most teams were made up of six people, the lead research analyst, and five assistants. There were a few projects that had only two people working on them and some with more than six. Mr. Bolin assigned the projects to the teams, and the leader of each team was responsible for completing a weekly project report detailing the work his team had completed. Mr. Bolin would go over all the reports and then meet with the team leaders as a group every other Wednesday. That way, each team leader could get direct feedback from the boss, and answer questions he might have. Just as important, that meant that each team leader could find out what all the projects were and how they were progressing. It was not uncommon for one team to have already encountered a situation another was now facing, and their insight was invaluable.

Gene Windom's death had left his team one short. Doug Malcolm had been promoted to team leader on Friday. It was this team that Debra was gravitating to, and she spent more time with them than any of the others. They had the Cold-X project that was nearing completion and another project, tentatively called "In-stent" which involved researching different ways to treat heart stents to keep scar tissue from developing. Doug explained that a stent is like a coiled wire; similar to what the wire spring in a ballpoint pen looks like.

This coil is placed in heart arteries when there is blockage from plaque. The surgeon is able to clean out the artery and insert the stent by going through an artery in the groin, thus avoiding invasive heart surgery. The problem is that over thirty percent of people who received heart stents developed scar tissue around the stent within six months of surgery, sometimes blocking the artery to a greater degree than it had been before, and the process had to be redone. Sometimes this would happen multiple times and eventually the patient might have to have open-heart surgery. Assuming he lived through the stent blockage. This team had a third project, "REFLEX," which was pretty much coming to a halt, after many years and a ton of money had been spent. Debra could tell this was something that was very disappointing to the team, and did not pursue the matter.

Mary and Debra returned to Mary's desk and found Greg Bolin waiting in his office for them. "Good morning, Mary, Debra. How was your tour?"

"It was very informative. You have a lot of interesting projects going on, and some really nice people. I'm excited to be here."

"You are right on both counts. Did you get a feeling about where you would like to start?"

"Well, the project that Doug Malcolm is heading up, researching the heart stents sounded really good to me. But, I'll go anywhere you like. The breast cancer research project is also interesting."

Bolin thought for a minute. "Well, Doug's team is short, and that project is just getting started good. That's probably a good fit. There isn't much left to do on the Cold-X project, and REFLEX is pretty much dead, so most of their efforts will be concentrated on In-Stent. I'll also be assigning the team another project soon; we are just working out some parameters now."

He walked across the room and selected two large three ring binders from a group of others and handed it to Debra. "Here, these are the weekly project reports on the Cold-X and In-Stent projects. They will help bring you up to speed. I'm sure Doug is working on the updates now, so you better take these. Remember, though, they cannot leave the research area. All of this information is very sensitive, and we have to be sure it does not fall into the wrong hands. Just get them back to me after you have looked them over."

"Yes sir. Thank you. I won't keep them long."

"Mary, why don't you take Debra back down to Doug's area and let them know she will be working with them. Doug will make sure she has a good desk and everything else she needs to get started. Tell him I'll get with him later."

-31-

J im Wooten went to his room at the hotel, shed his clothes and put on jeans, tennis shoes and jersey shirt. He felt the need for a little exercise, which, other than golf, was foreign to him. But, he enjoyed Washington with its traffic and beautiful buildings and so many landmarks. He took a couple of hours to just walk around and enjoy the sights, trying not to think about the people probably still meeting in the conference room, who were actually deciding the fate of his company and did not even know it. It was amazing that one drug could use up so many resources and be such a complete bust. Oh, they would survive, even without Cold-X, but they would have to file for bankruptcy, and it would be a long struggle.

The sun was bright, and there were throngs of tourists, and he thoroughly enjoyed this outing. He liked Washington because there was so much power in one place. He visited the space flight museum and was amazed again at the tremendous progress that had been made since the Wright brother's flew that first plane at Kitty Hawk. Pioneers in space had changed the world, and he admired that. Medicine is another area where progress has been as amazing as that of flight, he thought. And I am a pioneer in that field. Yes, I've taken risks, and yes, SARS is a terrible thing. But, just like the people who died in the quest to reach outer space, the people who died from SARS were making a tremendous contribution to mankind. Their deaths would enable Cold-X to be available much sooner than otherwise possible, saving many thousands of lives. He felt very good about himself as he walked back to the hotel.

He took a long shower and put on a fresh suit. He did not know where George Champion was taking him for supper, but he knew it would be someplace nice and expensive. He poured himself bourbon from the silver flask he carried when he traveled, and stood at the window watching the tourists, smoking his cigar and sipping his drink. The phone rang and the front desk clerk told him that Mr. Champion was waiting for him in the lobby.

"Hello, Jim. I know I'm a little bit early, but we have been invited to join Lynn Means and her husband for supper at her country club, if that is alright with you."

"That sounds good. It is not often that you get to dine with the White House Chief of Staff and her chief assistant. I hope this is an omen of good things to come."

Champion laughed. "Well, I wouldn't be surprised, but I don't know anything for sure. Let's go. I'm ready for a drink."

The men left, and Champion drove the Mercedes quickly through the streets of downtown and over the bridge into Virginia. He turned into an unmarked driveway on a street of stately mansions. The driveway wound its way through manicured landscaping and huge trees that blocked the view from the street. He pulled under a covered portico, and their doors were opened for them. A valet took the car keys.

"Good evening, Mr. Champion, Mr. Wooten. Mr. and Mrs. Means are already here. Let me show you to their table," said a distinguished black man dressed in an impeccable tuxedo, as if they were both regulars here. Wooten was very impressed, and he knew that was intentional.

All the tables were set apart with plants or furniture separating them, the idea being to provide more privacy than seating. They were shown to a table not unlike the others. Adam Means stood to shake hands as Champion made the introductions.

"Well, Mr. Wooten. I understand that you have created quite a stir. That's not always easy in this town."

Wooten did not know how to reply to that, so he just gave a short laugh and sat down. He turned to Lynn Means and asked, "How did it go today?"

"It was...interesting. Let's talk after we order." She nodded to the waiter standing discreetly by. "Johnny, I'll bet these gentlemen would like a cocktail."

The waiter stepped forward and took their order. The four talked briefly about the beautiful weather they had been experiencing while they waited on their order. The waiter returned with the four fresh drinks in over-sized glasses. He also brought a small tripod and set it up. He placed a large, hand printed menu on the stand that listed three entrees and described how each was prepared and the dishes that came with it. He placed a small device resembling a digital pager on the table.

"I won't disturb you further. Just press the button if you want more drinks or when you are ready to order." He gave a short bow and was gone.

Wooten said, "Now that is the kind of waiter I like. I hate being interrupted every five minutes while they check on you."

"Yes, they are very good about that here. That's why I come. That and the food. It is always delicious, and the menu changes daily. You can't order a bad meal here. Just doesn't exist." She paused and leaned forward. "Jim, I think we are going to be able to comply with your requests, for several reasons. I'm not going to promise you anything tonight, but I think I can have a commitment for you in a couple of days. Let me give you the lay of the land."

She paused to sip her drink. "Your drug, if it can cure SARS and the common cold the way all your tests indicate, is not only a wonderful medical development, it has huge diplomatic ramifications. Right now, the United States, as you know, is viewed by many as just a giant greedy country out solely for its own good. Being able to provide a cure like this to the world will be major. Especially right now with China. We have been undergoing some pretty sensitive trade negotiations with them. But SARS has put everything on hold over there. You just can't imagine what it has done to that country. People are dying; they are afraid to go to work; afraid to leave their apartments. Their economy is a total wreck, and it is affecting other

Fatal Healing

economies as well. This could solve all of that. I can tell you, the President is very excited about it, too."

"Well, then, what is the problem?"

"Joan Hadley over at FDA is a little reluctant to by-pass regular procedures. Don't get me wrong. She has not said 'no;' she just hasn't said, 'yes,' yet. She wants to be sure she isn't setting some kind of precedent. She will come around. I think the President will explain the bigger picture to her, if necessary."

"How long do you think it will take?"

"Another day or so. How long before your company can be in a position to provide the drug on a mass scale?"

"Oh, that is one beauty of this thing. It's a one shot deal. One pill and about forty-eight hours later, you are done. It's not like you take two every two hours. Fifty pills treat fifty people. We can be ready to distribute in a matter of days."

Adam Means joined in. "You are absolutely going to clean up with this. You will make a mint!" he exclaimed admiringly.

Wooten paused and took a long sip on his drink. "I surely hope so. That is why I'm in business. This one will make up for a lot of R&D money that has been wasted on drugs that did not pan out." He raised his glass in a toast. "Here's to success!" They all raised their glasses and drank.

Lynn suggested they order and signaled the waiter with the electronic pager. They all opted for the pecan-crusted grouper, stuffed with shrimp and lobster meat. The waiter took their order and brought them all fresh drinks without being asked.

George Champion turned to Wooten. "Jim, I know that we haven't given you the official go ahead, but it won't be but a few days. I used to be embarrassed to ask for campaign contributions, but I got over that. We do good things for this country and the world and even for individuals like you, and we can't do that if we aren't in office. It is very expensive to be here and to stay here. You know that. So just give it some thought. You have always been generous to us in the past, and we appreciate that."

"Don't worry about that. The check is already written. I appreciate having good people in control, and I want to do what I can to keep you here." He raised his glass, and they toasted again.

The waiter brought them each a spinach salad with pecans and strawberries, and they continued to talk as they ate.

Jim looked at Lynn, "What is your best guesstimate about this? How long before I get the preliminary approval, and how long before we take them the drug? What are the mechanics of it?"

"Jim, I think that we will have your approval before the week is out. Basically, you will have a written commitment from the FDA that if your drug performs in actual use as indicated in the tests, you will be given immediate FDA approval. I suspect they will want to watch the results for several months. After that, you can go full steam ahead. The President himself will inform the Chinese government about it and help pave the way for its immediate use. I suspect there will be lots of publicity about it after it has been proven effective, say in about two or three months. So, get ready for some television appearances. Of course, we will couch this as the United States, in conjunction with the Condor Corporation, has provided the cure."

"Of course," said Wooten. He did not really care who took the credit just so he got to take the money.

The meal lived up to all expectations. They each had an after dinner drink, and then Lynn Means signed the check. They exited the building to find their cars already waiting for them. They all shook hands and said goodnight.

Lynn Means said, "George will contact you in the next day or so, Jim. You may as well go home and not worry about it. You have hit a home run."

"Thank you Lynn. I appreciate all of your help. I look forward to hearing from you." And it's more like I hit a grand slam, he thought to himself.

George dropped him off at the hotel and promised to call him as soon as anything was finalized. Jim promised to send the contribution check as soon as he got home. He went to his room, poured another drink and lit another cigar. It was a celebration. He called and made arrangements for his return flight.

Jim Wooten left Washington on Tuesday morning and was back at his home on Lake Spivey before lunch. He decided he would take the rest of the day off, but called his office to check his messages. There were several routine items his secretary had handled, and one from Greg Bolin marked "important." He called Bolin and caught him before he left for lunch.

"Greg, this is Jim Wooten. What is going on?"

"I just wanted you to know that Detective Nebra came back out here yesterday, and questioned all the people Gene worked with. Tim and I sat in on the interviews, and there was nothing to it. But after he left, Nebra calls on the phone and asks me if I know anything about a SARS conference in Hong Kong. Gene had written it on the same paper that he had written 'Balium equals SARS.' I'm worried about what other surprises he has, Jim."

There was a long silence on the line and then Wooten spoke. "I'm not real happy to have the guy still snooping around, either. But I think he is just fishing. If he really had anything, he'd have search warrants. But words about SARS and a conference in Hong Kong don't mean anything, and it wouldn't be unusual for any of our researchers to have notes like that. It just means they are thinking. Just hang in there. This is all going fine. I just got back from Washington, and I think we will be in a position to start distributing Cold-X in China next week. We are going to be okay."

"Okay, boss. I guess there is nothing to do but wait. Anyway, that's why I called. Congratulations on your trip to Washington."

The men hung up and Wooten decided to take a boat ride around the lake.

-32-

Debra Raines spent the rest of the week getting acclimated to her new job and settling into a routine. As with most new jobs, it was very interesting and challenging. She was pretty sure this job would stay that way. She could not have been more pleased with the company or the people she worked with. She had talked to her father after his phone call last Friday, and he was planning to come see her tomorrow and Sunday. She was really looking forward to seeing him and rebuilding their relationship. Jack had called and taken her out to eat on Wednesday and had also asked her out for tonight. They were going bowling with Mike and Jen. She was excited about seeing them again. Everything seemed to be going her way.

♦♦♦

Jack Nebra spent Tuesday and Wednesday on stand-by for his testimony about the death of little Jamal, and did not get much else accomplished. On Thursday, he met with Detective Smith in his office.

How was the trial, Jack?"

"They convicted him. I think he'll get the death penalty, but he might get life without parole. Either way, he's out of here. Bring me up to date on the Windom case. What have you found out?"

"I think you are right. Rex Slaton sure looks suspicious right now. He bought the fishing boat at Shamrock Marine. They said he paid cash for it. Just over ten grand. He banks at SunTrust, and they wouldn't let me look at his account without a court order of course, but they did say there had not been any unusual activity in his account. His wife is an elementary school teacher and between them they make about seventy-five a year. They live pretty much pay check to pay check, I think. They have a nice house, two cars and a truck, and now a boat. I think it would be tough for him to come up with ten grand in cash - unless he borrowed it. SunTrust said he did not take out a loan with them. They've got one son, seventeen years old and a good kid - plays tight end on the football team over at Douglas High. Never been in trouble. I hope we are wrong about Rex. It would really hurt a kid like that to see his dad hauled off too prison."

"Yeah, but it is pretty tough on Windom's kids, too. They will never see him again. I'm going to see the D.A. I think we've got enough to get a court order to search Slaton's house and car and subpoena bank records. I assume that you did not find anything on any of the people that worked with Windom?"

"No. They were all clean. We probably have more things on our records to be suspicious of than they do. They are all top-notch."

"That is what I expected. So Slaton is still our only real suspect. I will call the DA right now."

"Okay. We had a convenience store robbery yesterday, and I'll be working on that. Believe it or not, they actually had a video camera that worked, so I'll be going over the film, if you need me."

"Anybody hurt?"

"They roughed up the clerk some, but at least, they didn't kill him. It was two black guys, both tall and skinny. Not much of a description - the store manager is from India, and it's a little hard to understand him."

"Okay, let me get this started, and I'll catch up with you."

Detective Smith left, and Jack called the District Attorney. He spoke to his secretary, who told him to come on over; he could meet with him now. The D.A.'s office is located in the courthouse in Douglas County. Jack left the police headquarters and walked the short distance to their office. He always admired the courthouse architecture. It was a three-story building of brick and granite with wide sweeping steps in the front, ten-foot high ceilings, and wide ten inch crown moldings throughout. It wasn't a modern building; it was timeless. The D.A.'s offices were on the third floor, and Jack took the steps two at a time.

He entered the reception area and was greeted warmly by the receptionist, who always looked forward to Jack's visits. She wished he were there to see her, but knew that was not the case.

"Hello, Jack. Go on back. Janice said that you were on the way over. You must have flown!"

"Yeah, I left my cape outside. Thanks, Margaret." He entered the offices of District Attorney Daryl Warren walked past several small offices and a conference room and finally reached his destination.

Janice Pilgrim smiled at him, she enjoyed Jack's visits too; he was an uncommonly good-looking man she thought now. I'm married, but I'm not dead. I can still look.

"Go on in, Jack. He's waiting for you."

Daryl Warren's office was one of the nicest that Jack had been in. It was a corner office with rows of windows looking out over the courthouse lawn. Its occupant was a local legend who had been in his elected post for years. No one ever even ran against him now. The job was his for as long as he wanted it, and this was not a bad thing. Daryl had great power, which he never abused, and he was well respected by the judges and defense lawyers. He rarely tried a case himself anymore, but if he did, the defense lawyers would immediately start making plans for an appeal, because the trial outcome was pre-ordained. He thought that Jack Nebra was the best detective that Douglasville had ever had.

"Hey, Jack. Come on in and sit down. What can I do for you?"

Jack told him about Windom's murder. He detailed the evidence they had accumulated and concluded by saying they needed to get a search warrant for Slaton's house, office and cars and financial records.

"So you are basing all this on a tight pattern of bullet holes and this guys reputation as a sharpshooter and the fact that he bought a new boat with cash? Is that the motive? You think he is a hired killer? Who do you think hired him?"

"Daryl, I don't have all the answers yet, and when you put it that way, it sounds a little thin. But, yes. Windom was shot while he was prone on the floor trying to shoot his own gun. It was dark, so the killer had to hold a flashlight with one hand and shoot with the other. There aren't very many people in the country who can shoot like that, and Slaton can. He knew the victim, because they worked at the same company; and all of a sudden he comes up with ten thousand cash to buy the boat. The sales people at Shamrock marine said he and his son came by all the time and looked at boats, but never bought. Then he just shows up and pays cash. It is all too coincidental. I'm just asking for a search warrant, not an arrest warrant."

"Okay, Jack. I'll go with you on this. But I want you to keep me informed. Before you go traipsing into The Condor Corporation with a search warrant for his office, I want to get back together with you. That company is big and powerful and accounts for a significant portion of this counties' tax base. I want to use kid gloves there. You search the house and vehicles and look at his financial stuff first. If we have enough, we'll go to Condor, but I want to look at and hear about what you find first. Understood?"

" No problem, sir. I can live with that."

"Okay. You know the procedure. Fill out the form and give it to Janice. I'll see if I can get Judge Davenport to sign it this afternoon or in the morning. You'll have it by tomorrow afternoon."

"Thanks, Daryl. I'll keep you informed about what happens," Jack said as he stood up to leave.

"Jack, be careful on this one."

"I will. Promise."

-33-

Alice Slaton, Rex Slaton's wife, was troubled. She had been married to Rex for twenty years and felt like she knew her husband well. Theirs was a pretty simple life. They both made fair money and had been able to afford a nice house and good vehicles. They did not have any savings, except for his 401k and her retirement plan, but they were comfortable. Their son, Greg, was an only child, and had never disappointed them. He made good grades and excelled in sports. The three got along well and enjoyed each other's company. It was a life that suited her perfectly.

She had known for some time her husband wanted a fishing boat, and that he would probably get one after Greg graduated from college, and their expenses were down. He and their son would visit the boat dealership from time to time and would talk for hours about the different boats. There was no harm in dreaming, she had thought often. But then, Rex had come home with that boat last Friday. He told her he had received this huge bonus from Condor. He even showed her almost five thousand in cash he promised to put in savings for Greg's education, thinking that would please her. She had been too shocked to speak. Then their son had come home and was so excited about the boat that she had to laugh with them. Monday had been a school holiday, and the two left early Sunday morning and went to the river for two days.

She stayed home and pondered things in her mind. She did not know where Rex had gotten the money, but she did not believe the bonus story. She knew that a company like Condor would not give out fifteen thousand dollars in cash as a bonus. What about accounting and taxes? But the boys had come home with a whole cooler of fish and were as excited as she had ever seen them. She said nothing

The week passed uneventfully, and now they had gone fishing again, just not over-night this time. Alice was beginning to believe she might have to learn to enjoy fishing, if she was going to get to see her son. She was still troubled about the money, but Rex seemed like his normal self, and did not appear to be worried about anything. If she had done something wrong to get fifteen thousand dollars, she would be petrified someone would catch her. Maybe it really was a bonus. Maybe they did give him a check, and he just cashed it. She did not believe that, but it helped to settle the matter for her. She was still troubled, but at least she did not dwell on it. She busied herself cleaning the house and ironing and doing all those things you still have to do even when things are not exactly right with your life.

♦♦♦

Rex Slaton was on top of the world. Alice had been upset about the boat when he first brought it home, because she did not know how they were going to pay for it. But she had gotten over it once he explained everything. He and his son had spent Sunday and Monday fishing on the Chattahoochee, and the trip had been all he had imagined it would be. They spent an hour cleaning the boat when they got home and put it in the garage, where his car used to be. His son was excited and happy, and that pleased Rex to no end.

Now they were back on the river, just floating and fishing. He watched the boy expertly cast his lure so that it settled softly in the water exactly where he wanted it. He opened another beer and then laughed with delight when he saw his son's pole bend as a large mouthed bass hit his lure. Greg fought the fish for several minutes until it tired, and then he reeled it in. Rex scooped the fish from the water with the net. It was about two and a half pounds. Good eating size. Life was wonderful, he thought again, as they floated. He used the trolling motor occasionally to steer them to areas that looked especially good. He was perfectly content to sit and watch his son. He was very proud he had been able to buy this boat so he could spend this quality time with him.

Rex gave not a thought to Gene Windom and his daughters. He had no clue his own life was about to change drastically. This son he was so proud of might soon have cause to no longer be very proud of him.

They fished the rest of the afternoon. It was a sunny, lazy day with only a few wisps of clouds and no breeze. Both were shirtless and the sun felt good on their bare skin. Each landed three nice sized bass, but Rex won the dollar that they had bet on the biggest fish, with one that weighed almost four pounds. It was close to seven o'clock when they got back to the boat ramp. Rex waited in the boat while his son expertly backed the trailer down the ramp. It was a drive-on trailer, and it only took a minute to secure the boat. Greg pulled the boat and trailer out of the river and away from the ramp. Rex pulled the plug on the boat, and they were on their way home by seven-fifteen.

-34-

Debra and Jack and Mike and Jen went bowling at the Starflight Bowling Center. There was not a lot to do in the small town of Sylvester, but bowling was available, and Debra had bowled quite often in her teen years. This bowling center was unlike any she had ever seen. Twenty-four lanes, psychedelic lights, a restaurant, music. The little eight- lane bowling alley in Sylvester could not claim any of these.

They rented their shoes and were given a number. A short while later, they were called and assigned a lane for a two-hour period. Debra was amazed at this, as well. In Sylvester it was first come, first served, and you just bowled until you were ready to quit. Here, there was so much demand that you were allowed only an allotted amount of time. Jack told her that it was not always this way, just some nights and on weekends. The others were all amazed at Debra's skill. She out-scored her new friends by at least twenty points.

Mike and Jen asked Debra how her first week on the job had been. The conversation turned naturally to the murder of the research associate and to Jack's investigation of the murder.

Jack looked at Debra and asked, "Have you noticed anything unusual at Condor? Anyone acting stressed or anything?"

Debra knew this was not a casual question, and she gave it some thought. "Well, yesterday, everyone I work with was talking about their meeting with you and Mr. Bolin and Mr. Murray. They were all naturally a little nervous before it was their turn to go, but nothing unusual."

"What about Greg Bolin, has he seemed nervous or upset?"

"I've really only seen him once, and that was on Monday. He seemed fine. Jack, why are you asking me this?"

"Debra, I'm sorry I can't just tell you everything. But, I think that Gene Windom was murdered by someone he knew, and I think it may come back to someone at Condor."

"Jack, you don't think Mr. Bolin did it?"

"No, no, I'm sorry. It's not him. It's just that the other day I asked him if there had been a SARS conference in Hong Kong, or if one was planned, and he told me no. I don't think he was being totally honest with me. I don't know why."

"What has SARS got to do with this?

Jack told them about the paper found in Windom's apartment. Mike and Jen were thrilled to know some of details of Jack's investigation, but he refused to talk about it any more. Mike obligingly changed the subject and talked about his students.

"If Theresa was here, they'd have to give her three lanes, just so she would have room to set up." He mimicked his student whose mother had the overweight friend, and they all laughed.

They enjoyed a wonderful evening together, and it ended too quickly. Jack had driven, and he dropped off Mike and Jen before taking Debra home. Debra asked him in and poured herself a glass of wine and Jack some orange juice.

"You do not drink at all, do you?"

"Not anymore, but don't worry, when I used to drink I consumed enough to last a lifetime. It cost me my job with the FBI. That woke me up, and I quit totally. I haven't had a drop in over three years. I don't think I am an alcoholic, because it did not even bother me to stop. I just got into the habit in college and kept going. I thought life was a big party. But you go ahead, it doesn't bother me for others to drink. Just know that I'll stop you if you drink too much."

"My limit is one or two glasses of wine a week, so don't worry about that. I tried one of my Dad's beers one time. He gave it to me so I would know what it was like. It was awful. I did not know you worked for the FBI. So did my dad."

"Yeah, I remember that. He is coming tomorrow, isn't he?"

"He should get here around noon. Debra paused, then continued. "Jack, about that note you found at Windom's house. I've been reading the weekly progress reports on one of our drugs, and balium is a manufactured chemical that is used in it."

"Yeah, Bolin told me that, said this drug would be used to treat the common cold, and Windom was probably just wondering if it could treat SARS. I can buy that. It's the conference thing that I'm puzzled about. I just had the feeling that it bothered Bolin when I asked about it. I may be wrong. I haven't seen anything to indicate he was involved in this. He was for sure surprised when he found out about the murder."

"But you think someone at Condor is."

"Well, maybe. There are a few things that bother me about one guy. There is no real proof, but there was enough to get a search warrant for his house and vehicles. We'll serve it sometime on Monday, and know more after that. Let's talk about something else. Tell me about your family. Your Dad sounds like a good guy. What about your Mom?"

Jack knew he had brought up a subject that was painful to Debra when her eyes welled with tears. He reached out and touched her hair.

"Hey, I'm sorry. I didn't know this was a bad subject." Debra wiped her eyes with her thumb and forefinger. "It's not a bad subject. I'm sorry. It's just that my mother was killed in a car wreck a few years ago. We were all very close. But dad kind of shut me out for a while. I guess we all deal with grief in different ways. That hurt a lot. Lately, we have been in touch more. This will be our first real visit in a good while. I guess I'm a little apprehensive about it. Excited, too. I love my dad, he really is the kindest and smartest man I've ever met."

"What are your plans for while he's here?"

Debra looked at Jack and said, "That is a good question, I haven't even thought about that. I guess we'll just visit and spend time together. I'll take him out and show him where I work and all. He used to live here so he'll probably want to drive around some areas he used to go. We'll go to the park and walk around. Then, I'll fix him a home cooked meal. He probably eats out all the time now. Would you like to come eat with us?"

"Are you sure?" I don't want to barge in on your time together."

"Yes, I'm sure. I'd like you to meet him, and we may need a referee by that time," she joked. "Plan on coming over about 6:30. We'll eat at seven. And come hungry. I haven't had a real home cooked meal in a while either, so I'm going to do it up."

"Okay, I'll be here. Now, I'd better go so we can both get some sleep."

He stood to leave and Debra walked him to the door and thanked him for a wonderful evening. This was the part she hated. It was always awkward when they said goodnight. She wished he would go ahead and kiss her and get that out of the way. They had been out four times already, and he had only kissed her on the forehead. As they reached the door, she put her hand on his shoulder, and he turned and kissed her on the mouth. Twice. Long. Then they hugged.

Jack opened the door and said softly "Goodnight, Debra. Lock up. I'll see you tomorrow." He walked to his car and drove home feeling very good about this relationship.

Debra locked up and smiled. Wow. That was nice. So much for the awkwardness. She was a happy girl.

-35-

Police Chief Bob Raines drove ten miles an hour over the speed limit on I-75 northbound heading for Atlanta. He had to, or risk causing a wreck. Cars zoomed past him constantly, and he wondered, where was the state patrol? Actually, he knew there were so few officers and so many drivers, they could only go after the worst violators. He thought about the trooper in Valdosta, who ticketed a person driving the speed limit for "impeding traffic." Bob was sure the man was trying to make a point. If you are going to allow people to drive eighty, then change the speed limit. Stop selective enforcement. Bob liked that kind of officer.

It was an uneventful trip, and traffic was light on Saturday mornings. He followed Debra's instructions, and found her apartment without any problem. He was both excited and nervous, as he knocked on her door. It was strange, knocking on your own daughter's door like she was some stranger, he thought. Debra opened the door and smiled at him and his heart went to his throat. Lord, he had missed her! He stepped inside, and they hugged each other for a long time, enjoying the closeness they had been without for too long.

"Thanks for coming, Dad. It is really good to see you. I've missed you."

"I've missed you, too. I'm sorry it has been so long. How are you, Deb?"

They talked for several minutes before Debra showed him to his room. He put his things away and joined her back downstairs. She was putting the marinating beef tenderloin back into the refrigerator.

"Hey, Deb. This is a really nice place. I like the way you have your apartment decorated. This looks like a great area, too. I'm proud for you." He wanted to know how much it cost to rent each month, but wisely left that alone.

"Thanks, Dad. I'm still getting settled in, but I do like it. Especially the garage at the end of the building. Now I can keep my car out of the weather. Speaking of which, it is beautiful outside. Why don't I make us a picnic lunch, and we'll go to the park and eat, then walk around some?"

"Whatever you say, beautiful. That sounds great."

Debra made three BLT sandwiches and put chips and drinks in a cooler, and they were off. She insisted they drive her Miata, with top down. Once he got over how tiny the car was, her dad loosened up and enjoyed the ride. The weather was perfect, and it was just a short drive to the public park. Debra spread a tablecloth on one of the picnic tables, and they enjoyed a quiet lunch and conversation. Later, they walked around the jogging trail, which was almost exactly one mile. They loaded up in the convertible and drove by the Condor Corporation, so she could show her dad where she worked. From there they drove downtown, and he showed her his old work place. And they just explored and enjoyed the ride and savored their time together. They talked as she drove, and she told him about Gene Windom's murder, and how she had to take a day off work before she even started.

"That's exactly what worries me about you living here. People are just so mean; drugs are so available; and traffic is horrible. It scares me. I mean someone just picks this guy's house, breaks in and kills him, and for what, some drug money?"

"I'm sure that happens sometimes, but Jack seems to think this was not a random killing. In fact, he thinks someone at Condor might be involved."

Her Dad turned his whole body in the seat to look at her. "Well, that sure gives me the warm fuzzies. Who is Jack, and what do you mean someone at Condor might be involved?"

Debra looked at her father and patted his hand. "It's okay, Dad, relax. Jack is a guy that I have been out with several times. In fact I invited him over for supper tonight. I'm going to fix us a really good meal. And no, it's not serious, at least not yet. Anyway, Jack is a detective for Douglas County, and he is in charge of the investigation. He just told me that someone at Condor is a suspect, and they are going to search his house on Monday."

"What else did he say about it?"

"Nothing, he doesn't want to talk about an active case. Neither would you."

Her dad sat back straight in his seat. He was not sure he liked anything he had heard in the last little bit. They got back to the townhouse about five and freshened up. Debra began to prepare their evening meal, while her dad channel surfed the various news stations. He recognized Mia Munson on NewsNow and called out to Debra.

"Hey, isn't this one of your sorority sisters?"

Debra walked around the corner to look. "Yes, that is Mia Munson. She is prettier than ever, don't you think?"

"Yeah, she's pretty, but not as pretty as you. She's high maintenance, and you are just a natural beauty. Do you ever talk to her?"

"No, I haven't talked to her in years."

"Why don't you give her a call sometime? It's nice to keep in touch with friends."

"You are right. Maybe I will."

Jack arrived at exactly 6:30. Debra made the introductions and told them to get acquainted while she finished their meal. The aroma from the beef tenderloin had both men anxious to help, but she told them to just sit down and let her finish.

"Debra tells me that you are a cop too, a detective?"

"Yes sir. I guess we have that in common. I understand that you are a police chief and ex-FBI. I am too. I was with them six years before coming to Douglasville."

"Really? Debra didn't tell me that. What is this about someone at her work possibly being involved with a murder?"

"Well right now, that is just a suspicion of mine based on some of the evidence. We do not have any real proof yet."

"But you have enough to get a search warrant?"

"Yes. We will serve it Monday."

"What kind of evidence do you have?"

Jack hesitated. It went against all he had been taught to discuss an open investigation with someone that did not have a need to know. But this was a man he very much wanted to be on his side, not against him; and after all, he was a police officer. He would be leaving here tomorrow, anyway. Also, he might even be able to offer insight. Bob Raines waited patiently for Jack to answer. He pretty much knew what Jack was thinking and would not be offended if he chose not to discuss the case. But he hoped he would.

Finally, Jack said, "I will tell you what I know because of who you are, but I would appreciate it if what I say stays right here."

"Fair enough."

"Well, the man that was killed was shot by a person with great skill." Jack told Bob all about the crime scene, and how the bullet wounds were so close together. "Then we find out the security chief at Condor is that good a marksman. Even served on the World Pistol Team, representing the Army. Then we found out he purchased a new boat, for cash, right after the murder. It was an extravagant purchase for him. From all we can determine, he and his wife make enough to get by, but not to have ten grand lying around. We also found out he had served on the APD (Atlanta Police Department) for ten years and had a couple of unnecessary roughness charges filed against him. The last one was really bad. It cost him his job."

"Well, you are right. It all looks suspicious, but it could be nothing. It isn't a crime to be a good shot, and for all you know, the man's father died and left him some money."

"Yeah, I know. But it's too much to ignore. We have to check it out."

"Right. Do you have anything else?"

"A few things. There was glue residue from duct tape on the front door where the intruder taped a magnet to get by the alarm sensor. And the door lock had been picked. There were no computer discs, and we know from his wife that there had been a box of them. And then there was this piece of paper with doodling on it. That is all we were able to get from the crime scene."

"What was on the paper?"

"It said, 'balium equals SARS conference equals Hong Kong.' The equal was not spelled out - just the math sign for equal was on it."

"Do you have any idea what that means?"

Debra interrupted them. "Let's eat, guys."

Both men had been able to see her putting food on the table, and they were ready. Besides the beef tenderloin, which was cooked to perfection, she had small butter peas, mashed potatoes and gravy, rolls, salad and sweet tea. And peach cobbler for desert. It all looked and smelled delicious. Jack held her chair for her, and then the men sat down,

"Dad, will you say grace?"

They all ate more than they should. Jack and Bob told Debra several times that it was the best meal they had ever eaten, and

Debra was all smiles. After it was over, they all worked together to clear the table, clean the dishes and put things away. They settled down in the living room, perfectly content.

"What were you two talking about all that time? Ya'll were pretty engrossed."

"Jack was telling me a little about the murder investigation, just cop stuff."

Jack said, "Sir, I can answer your question about that paper. Debra already knows about it. The balium equals SARS is simple enough. Balium is a chemical that Condor is using in a drug to fight colds, and he was probably wondering if it could help with this SARS thing. But, according to her boss, there was no SARS conference in Hong Kong, nor is one planned."

Bob Raines digested this and thought for a moment. "Did it say 'SARS conference' or just 'conference?'"

Jack said, "You know what? You are right. It just said conference. I just assumed the SARS part because it was mentioned."

Bob grinned, happy he had helped. They decided to walk around the complex and let their food settle. The case was not mentioned again.

At eleven Jack said, "I guess I'd better go so we can all turn in. Are you going back tomorrow, Mr. Raines?"

"Yes, Debra is taking me to church, and then I'll head back after lunch." He pulled out his billfold and removed a business card. He wrote his cell number on the back. "Here, take this in case you ever need to get in touch with me. You take care of my daughter, please. I worry about her, even if she is grown."

"Yes sir, I will. It was really nice to meet you. I hope to see you again soon." The men shook hands, and Debra walked Jack to the door. He thanked her again for the wonderful meal, kissed her and left.

Debra's dad told her what a fine young man Jack seemed to be; and they talked for another thirty minutes before turning in for the night.

-36-

Jim Wooten had only been to his office once since his return from Washington. He had the brief conversation with Bolin, but had not spoken to the others. So, Monday morning Wooten, Bolin, Murray, and Horton all met in Wooten's office. Wooten told them about the trip to Washington.

"This is working out even better that I thought. I had not considered the diplomatic angle of this. But it really gives them an incentive to help us. They want the United States to come across as a benevolent benefactor to the world, and hopefully get rid of some of the negative publicity about American greed. I expect to hear back from them this week; they are that excited. And, the timing could not be better. SARS is out of hand over there, and now it has hit Canada. They are going nuts. Do ya'll have any questions?"

"Not about that, Mr. Wooten," said Bolin, "but I guess we are still all a little uptight about that detective."

"I know. But I wouldn't worry about it. He can't have anything. I suspect he'll just fade away."

He was wrong.

Jack Nebra and Joel Smith went to see the Chief, search warrant in hand. He was already familiar with the case. Jack showed him the search warrant and told him they wanted to set up the search. There was discussion about the times someone would likely be home. Jack knew that Mrs. Slaton generally arrived home from her teaching job around four. The son had baseball practice and would not be home until late, to their relief. Rex Slaton generally arrived around 5:30. They did not want to forewarn him by calling him at work, and getting him to meet them there, so they decided to arrive at 5:45. The chief made arrangements for a Marshal and three other officers to accompany them.

It was going to be a long day. They had two suspects who had been brought in for questioning in the convenience store robbery, and a ton of paperwork, then the search. The day passed fairly quickly as Jack was kept busy watching the interrogation of the suspects and catching up on a number of items that had been on his desk for way too long.

At four o'clock the search team met in the conference room and Jack outlined the parameters of the search warrant. The men were all seasoned officers who had been involved in searches before, so the meeting did not take long. They were ready to leave by five o'clock.

-37-

M ary Hightower stopped by Debra's desk about 10:30 to ask if she had plans for lunch. She did not, so they decided to go somewhere together. It was overcast and drizzling when they left, so Mary got a reprieve on riding in the Miata. She drove to a nearby Atlanta Bread Company restaurant, and they each ordered clam chowder and a half sandwich.

"Debra, I enjoyed meeting your father at church yesterday. He seems like such a fine man. I'm so glad you came back to visit and brought him with you."

"We both enjoyed it. Dad could not get over how friendly people were. He said he talked to as many people yesterday as he does on Sundays at his church, and he has been a member there for almost thirty years. Ya'll really do have a great congregation."

"It could be your congregation too, Debra. We would love to have you become a regular member. I'm not pushing you. I just wanted you to know the invitation is there."

"Thanks, Mary, I know. I'll be thinking about it."

They talked about both their weekends, and Debra told her about the bowling date.

"It sounds like you and Jack are getting along pretty good. Is it serious, yet?"

"No, not yet. But it could be. He is really a terrific guy. Even Dad was impressed with him, and he never has been with anyone else I dated."

A thought occurred to Debra as they were driving back to work. "Mary, is there any kind of medical or pharmaceutical conference going on in Hong Kong?"

Mary glanced at her, "I doubt it. They just had one a while back, so I doubt they will have another any time soon. I think the next one is in Las Vegas, and it is over a year away."

"When did they have that one in Hong Kong?"

"It was three or four months ago. I remember because Gene Windom was planning to go, but Mr. Bolin decided he would go instead. I guess he just needed a little company vacation." she joked. She glanced over at Debra. "What is it, Debra? What's wrong?"

"Oh, my gosh. Nothing, Mary. I'm just surprised." She wouldn't say any more and Mary knew something was wrong, but had no idea what it might be.

When Debra got back to her office, she removed from her desk drawer the weekly progress report for Cold-X that Mr. Bolin had given her. She had read most of it, and she flipped back to the middle of the report and read it again, very carefully, all the way to the end. She put the book back in her drawer and looked at the clock. It was time to go home. She left the building and drove quickly home. Once there, she called Jack and left him a message to call her. She was not at all happy about what she was thinking. She fixed a light supper, because she really was not hungry. When Jack had not called her by eight, she called again, but hung up without leaving a message. He might have a date, she thought, not just a little apprehensively. Well, he was certainly free to do so. He had not made any commitment to her. But now she was bothered about that, too. She really needed to talk to someone.

"Hello, Dad, bet you didn't expect to hear from me so soon, did you?"

"No, I didn't," he laughed, "But I am delighted. What's up?"

"Dad, I found out some stuff at work today, and it is bothering me. I tried to call Jack, but he's not home."

"Talk to me."

Debra told him about the conference and about the contents of the progress report. It took her a while, because she had to keep stopping to explain things to her dad. If he wasn't absolutely sure about what she was saying, he made her explain.

When she finished, he asked: "You do know what you are suggesting, don't you?"

"Yes. It just sounds so bizarre and impossible. There may be lots about all this research I don't understand, but it sure looks suspicious with what I do know."

"Okay, now I am really worried about you. If what you are suggesting is true, then they have already killed one person because of that information. Don't you tell anyone about this but Jack, and then only in person. I really want you to stay away from work, but that might make them suspicious. Do you still have that .32 pistol I bought you?"

"Yes."

"Well, you keep it in your purse. I doubt anything will come up, but I want you to keep it with you, okay?"

"I will."

"Okay, try not to worry about it. Call me after you talk to Jack. I love you, Debra."

"I love you too, Dad."

Chief Raines sat by the phone for a long time after his daughter hung up. Years ago, he had left that area because he wanted to protect his family. Now his wife had been killed in a car wreck and his daughter was back in Atlanta and possibly in danger. He was the only one safe. It was not at all what he had in mind.

-38-

Jim Wooten's cell phone rang at two o'clock. The caller ID showed it was a Washington number, and Wooten's hopes instantly rose. When he answered, it was George Champion.

"Good afternoon, Jim. I have good news. Everything is set. I will fax you a copy of the FDA commitment in just a minute. How soon can you get a hundred samples of the drug and be back in Washington?

"Well, I can probably have that many by in the morning and be there tomorrow afternoon, if I needed to. Do I?"

"Maybe. We may want you to personally take them over to Hong Kong with several other folks, including the Vice President and the Chinese ambassador. The ambassador has already been brought up to speed, and it would be a real political deal for him if he could accompany the drug with you. Of course, there will be minimal publicity until they actually see it work and know there are no side affects. You said that took about forty-eight hours, right?"

"That's right."

"Well, everybody here had a chance to look at it, and there just isn't a downside to doing it. This is really a win-win for everyone. The fax should be there by now. Go ahead and gather the samples, and I'll call you back. I think that schedule for your arrival will work. Everyone is ready to do this. Oh, and Jim, thanks for the contribution. Very generous."

He called back in thirty minutes. "It is all set. Did you get your confirmation and is it satisfactory?"

"Yes, it's fine. What do I need to do?"

"Get the samples and come to Washington. You will leave here tomorrow around two. It will just be you three. You'll need to stay for about four days, to allow time for the drug to work, and there may be some preliminary press announcements. There will also be some meetings with high powered officials, can you manage that?"

"Yes. Are we leaving from Reagan field?"

"Yes."

"I'll just arrange to fly in about one-thirty. I guess you will be there?"

"Yes, I'll be there and introduce you to the others, and just make sure all is well. See you tomorrow."

The men hung up and Wooten called Greg Bolin. "We are on, Greg! I leave here in the morning - first to Washington and then to Hong Kong. I'll need about one hundred samples of Cold-X to take with me."

"That's great. A hundred will pretty much wipe us out, but we've got them. I'll bring them up in a few minutes. Do you need anything else?"

Wooten was just getting off the phone after making the flight arrangements with Smith Air, when Bolin came in with the pills. They talked for a few minutes, and Wooten told him he could let the others know about the latest developments. He had to leave now if he was going to get everything done that he needed to. They shook hands and an obviously elated Bolin left. Wooten and his secretary talked for a few minutes about items on his calendar that needed to be rearranged, and he left, as well.

Bolin went directly to Tim Murray's office to share the news. The men laughed and talked together for a little while and decided they would leave work a little early and play a few games of racquetball. Neither had played in a couple of weeks. Tim agreed to call Bill Horton with the news, and Greg went back to his office to wind things up for the day.

Bolin and Murray met in the lobby about twenty minutes later and waved to Rex Slaton, who was talking to one of the security officers. Rex had completed going over the daily reports and, having finished for the day, was also leaving early. He planned to stop by Wal-Mart and get a new trolling battery for the boat. The one he had was old, and he wanted a backup for this weekend in case they decided to go camping again.

-39-

J ack, Joel, a Marshal and three officers arrived at Slaton's home right on schedule. They came in three cars, but only the Marshal's was marked. Rex Slaton was in the garage wiping the dust off of his boat, and they could see each other through the open garage door. He walked slowly out to meet them, the dust rag still in his hand and an expression on his face that was both puzzled and a little frightened.

"What's going on?" he asked Nebra.

The Marshal stepped forward. "Are you Rex Slaton?"

"Yes"

"We have a warrant to search your house and vehicles, so just let us do our job without any trouble, and we'll be out of here." He handed Slaton a copy of the warrant. He took it and looked at Jack again.

"What is this all about? You can't think I had anything to do with this."

By this time one of the neighbors, who had just arrived home, had stopped his car in his driveway and was watching the proceedings with great interest. Alice Slaton was standing in the doorway, her hand at her mouth and a very sad expression on her face.

"Let's go inside and not cause a scene out here," Detective Smith suggested, and without comment they all walked toward the door.

Once inside, Jack introduced himself and the other officers to Alice Slaton.

"I'm sorry about this, Mrs. Slaton. But we have a search warrant. We will try not to mess things up too badly."

She could not reply. She could only look at her husband with anguish in her eyes.

Slaton was still full of bluster. "Look, detective, I have a right to know what is going on here. What are you looking for, and why?"

Jack answered, "Mr. Slaton there are some things about the Windom murder that we need to clear up, that seem to point to you. Now, if we are wrong, I apologize. Perhaps you can clear up those things for us."

"All you had to do was ask me. You have no call to barge in here and frighten my wife like this. Embarrass us in front of our neighbors. I'm glad our son isn't here. Now, tell me what you want, and I will see if I can help you."

Jack turned to the other officers. "Okay, y'all know what we are looking for. Look good, but be neat about it. Start in the house. Mrs. Slaton, you do not have to stay here if you would rather leave."

She just shook her head and sat on the couch. Jack turned back to Slaton. "You can start clearing things up by telling me where you got ten thousand dollars to buy the boat and another five thousand to open up the new savings account."

Dorothy put her hand to her mouth. Rex said simply. "It was a bonus."

"What kind of bonus, and for what?"

"How many kinds of bonuses are there? It was a bonus for doing good work all these years at Condor."

"Who gave it to you?"

"Mr. Wooten gave it to me. He said I had done really good work and to look at it as a scholarship for my son. But he's going to get a football scholarship, so I bought a boat with part of it. That ain't illegal."

"So, Condor gave you a bonus check, and you cashed it?"

"No, it was cash."

"Well, we'll talk to their accounting office tomorrow then, and that should clear that up. Where were you on the night of the 22nd, the night Windom was killed?"

"I was right here, and I don't think I'm going to answer anything else without a lawyer."

Jack shrugged his shoulders. "Suit yourself, I probably wouldn't either."

The officers spent several hours searching the house. At one point one of the officers showed Nebra a .22 pistol and a Glock pistol. He told the officer to leave them, there was nothing illegal about them, but to look for a .38 caliber pistol like was used in the murder. Slaton turned over the .38 he wore at work, and Jack put it into an evidence bag.

They took the computer and all floppy discs. When Rex said that was his son's computer, Jack apologized and said he would keep it no longer than necessary. They found nothing else in the house and moved to the garage and vehicles. It was here they found a powerful magnet about six inches long and two inches wide. They marked this and bagged it. Slaton, who was watching, told them he used it to pick up screws and other things he dropped when working on the cars. When they searched his vehicle they found two slender tools, about the size of tweezers. One had a flat end on it similar to a screwdriver and the other had a slight cup on its pointed end. Lock picking tools. Jack looked quizzically at Slaton as they also marked and bagged them.

"I have those in case someone accidentally locks a door at Condor. You'll also find a 'slim Jim' in there that I use to open car doors for employees who accidentally lock their keys in their car. So what?"

It was not until they found the single floppy disc between the console and the bucket seat that Slaton became nervous.

"I...I don't know whose that is, or where it came from."
Jack just looked at him, and they continued their search. Greg Slaton had come home about seven, and his mother had hurriedly taken him inside, but not before he could ask his dad what was going on. Rex had told him it was a mix-up of some kind and not to worry about it. Jack could tell that satisfied the son, but not Alice Slaton.

It was after eleven when they finally finished, and they still had to go back to headquarters and log everything in. Jack told Slaton not to leave town, and the officers left. It was after one Tuesday morning, before Jack got home. He figured it was too late to return Debra's call and he went to bed and slept until ten.

◆◆◆

By the time Jack got to the office, Jim Wooten was getting on a Leer jet headed for Washington. Debra was at work, doing her best to act normally. Mary sensed something was wrong when she talked with her briefly in the break room, but Debra told her everything was fine - that she just had a headache. She spent the day accomplishing a few minor tasks assigned to her, and going back over the Weekly Progress Report that Mr. Bolin had given her. In fact, she was going over it, when he appeared at her desk.

"Oh, Debra, I was hoping you were through with that. I need it for the meeting tomorrow, sorry."

"I am through with it. I was just refreshing my memory," she said as she handed him the book.

"Good. I hope everything is going well for you. I am hearing only good things about you. We really are glad to have you here."

He talked with her briefly about her work, then smiled warmly at her and left. He was so nice. Debra began to question herself. Surely there was another explanation. Something totally innocent. The research spanned several years and was very technical at times, using methods and means that Debra knew nothing about. There was way more here than someone with her limited experience could possibly understand. There were years and years of studies and notes, and here she was on the job less than two weeks, acting like she understood everything. But the report was clear, she had thought. Now, she was not sure. She felt badly and wished she had not called her father. At least she hadn't told Jack. Making accusations like that could cause her to lose her job. And Jack would probably think she was just some dumb girl jumping to conclusions. She really was very confused, and that was not a condition she was used to. She tried to concentrate on the work at hand. They were researching eight different methods of treating the heart stents to keep scar tissue from forming. There was plenty for her to do to keep her mind occupied.

-40-

Rex Slaton did not sleep very well at all, nor did his wife. Neither wanted to discuss the situation, so they both just lay there staring into the dark, each with their own thoughts. If he had known Mr. Wooten's unlisted number, he would have called him last night. He couldn't very well leave and go back to the office and get it without really causing a rift with his wife, so he had just waited. Besides, he was probably being watched, and he needed to act normally.

He arrived at the office early and called Wooten, who had obviously been wakened by the phone. "Mr. Wooten, this is Rex Slaton. I am sorry to bother you so early, but we've got a problem."

He proceeded to tell him about the search warrant, and what the police had taken, and their questions about the fifteen thousand dollars.

"How did they find out about the money?"

"I don't know, but they knew I had bought a boat with part of it and opened up a savings account with the rest."

"You what?" The words exploded from Wooten.

Rex repeated himself.

"Weren't you listening to anything I said? I told you not to buy anything big with it! Damn, you have really screwed up now."

"I'm sorry, Mr. Wooten, I guess I was so excited at the time that I don't remember that. I just remember you said to look at it like a scholarship. That's why I opened the savings account. And that is what I told them."

"What exactly did you tell them? Every word."

"They asked me where I got the money, and I told them it was a bonus for years of good work, and that you had given it to me. That it was like a scholarship for my son. They asked me if it was a check, and I told them no, that it was cash. Then they said they would check with accounting today and verify that."

Wooten uttered a string of expletives. "Rex, call me back in thirty minutes. I need to think about this."

He then got into the shower and let the hot water beat on his shoulders, and head. He wanted to be sure he was thinking very clearly. When Rex called back, he told him he would be at the office in a half hour, to just sit tight and not to talk to anyone. Fortunately, he had packed for his trip the night before. He loaded his suitcases in his car and drove to the office. When he crossed over the dam, he could see the skiers on the lake and shook his head, it was only 7:30. There was a blonde headed kid with them today, and he was skiing around the buoys in the ski course, his shoulders only inches above the water as he carved the turns.

Traffic was heavy at this time of morning, and the trip took him more than twice as long as normal, which did not ease his frustration level. But, it did give him time to further assess the situation. He just could not believe his security chief had been that stupid. He had let a disc get lost in his car, and he had gone and done exactly what Wooten had told him not to do with the money. He pounded the wheel and cursed.

From what Rex had told him, the money and the computer disc were the only incriminating things the cops had. There may or may not be anything on the disc that would link Slaton to Windom's house, but he still had the bag of discs that Slaton had given him, and there was surely something on at least one that would. He intended to dispose of them immediately, and could not think of any good reason he had not already done so. As far as the money went, Rex could not prove that it came from him. If nothing was on the disc they found in Rex's car, then the money wouldn't matter. Wooten could deny he had given him the money, and so what? Rex would have some money he couldn't explain, but they could not arrest him for that. But if he denied giving him the money, he would surely alienate his security chief. He was not ready for that yet, unless it was necessary. On the other hand, if something were on the disc that linked Rex to Windom, he sure as hell did not want the money to be tied to him. It all came down to the unknown. What was on the disc?

When he got to Condor, he went to his office and called Rex, telling him to come up. He then removed the discs from his floor safe. He broke them into pieces and put them back into the bag. Rex arrived and shut the door.

"I'm sorry, Mr. Wooten," he started, but Wooten held up his hand.

"Save it Rex. Right now we need to talk. If the cops find something on that disc that links you to Windom, they are going to arrest you. There is no way around that. Now, if that happens, I will figure a way to help you, hire an attorney, and make sure your family doesn't starve and all. But you could very well get some time. And I have no intention of joining you. I can better serve both of us if I am kept out of it. And if you try to drag me into it, you have no proof, and I will become your worst enemy. You do understand that, don't you?"

"Yes, sir. Don't worry. I would never say anything to hurt you. You have been too good to me."

"Rex, I don't want you to say anything at all. Nothing. Name, rank and serial number that is it. Now I am leaving the country today, and I will not be back for about a week. I will check in with my secretary, and if they do arrest you, she will let me know, and I'll see about getting you a lawyer. I will have to do that without anyone knowing it's me, though, and that might take a few days. What I am saying to you is that if they arrest you, you might be in jail for a while before I am able to help you. Do not say a word. If they appoint an attorney for you, don't tell him anything either. If you do, you are on your own. Understood?"

"Yes sir."

"Now about the money. They know you have it. We can't do anything about that now. If they find something on the disc, and they know the money came from me, then I'm right in there with you. So you need to forget where that money came from. You just got amnesia and you don't remember where you got it, but you did not get it from me, and you don't know why you told them that in the first place. Understood?"

"Yes, sir."

"On the other hand, if they don't find anything on the disc, they can't just arrest you. In that case, I may be able to confirm that I gave you a bonus, and we'll fix the books so it shows up that way. Then, you are home free. That is where my being out of the country is going to come in handy. They won't be able to ask me about it, and Bill Horton is going to tell them he just doesn't know whether I gave you a bonus or not. I have given bonuses in the past and told him about it later, so he can just plead ignorance. By the time I get back, we'll know where the chips lay. Either you will be in jail or you won't. The main thing is that you just don't talk to them at all. If they arrest you, just sit there like a big dummy and say nothing at all."

"Yes, sir."

Wooten regarded him for a moment and then gave him the bag of discs. "Take these down to the hazardous waste incinerator, and make sure they are burned up. You don't need to let anyone see you doing it, either."

Rex stood up and took the bag. "Yes sir, and I am really sorry about this."

"Okay Rex, I know. We will get through it. Maybe there is nothing on the disc they found, but if there is, remember that you want me on your side, not against you."

Rex assured him he understood and left. He took the bag of discs straight to the incinerator. There was rarely anyone around it, and this morning was no exception. He threw the discs into the roaring fire and left the steel door open as he watched the plastic curl in flames. He did not know how he had screwed up so badly, but at least Mr. Wooten was going to help him. He really was a good man.

Wooten called Bill Horton and asked him to come to his office.

"Bill, you may get a call from the police, probably that Detective Nebra, wanting to know if we gave Rex Slaton a fifteen thousand dollar bonus. Just tell them that you don't know, that I have given bonuses in the past and told you about it later so the books would reflect it properly. I'm leaving for Hong Kong in just a little while, so you won't be able to ask me about it until I get back."

Horton was more than a little flustered. "What has happened?" he managed to ask.

Wooten briefly explained the situation. "There is no way they can tie any money to me. It would just be his word against mine; and between you and me, I'll never say we gave him a bonus. This is just a way to find out if they have anything on him. Just plead ignorance. With all we have going on right now, we don't want even a hint of suspicion. It could screw up everything. Washington is looking at this as a big public relations deal, and it won't work if Condor is involved in something illegal - let alone murder."

"Do Greg and Tim know about this?"

"No, I haven't had time to talk with them. And I probably won't. There is nothing they can do about it."

Wooten arrived at Smith Air at noon, right on time. It only took a little over an hour to fly to Washington in the Leer.

-41-

Jack Nebra woke at ten in the morning and fixed breakfast. He read the morning paper and then went to the office. He was to meet Detective Smith at one o'clock to evaluate the case. They would look at all the evidence at that time. Jack was anxious to look at the computer discs they found, especially the one from the car. If any of the discs had any information at all linking them to Windom or Condor, this could be the clinching information they needed. He got to the office just before noon and went down to the evidence room to retrieve the computer and the discs they found in the house, as well as the one they found in the car. He put all of it on a cart and took it across the hall to a large room that was set up with several tables and a large computer monitor and a series of wires for hooking up any kind of computer equipment. He had called Tim Wilson, who was the in-house computer expert, and he was going to meet them at one o'clock as well. He normally did not drink coffee after eleven, but he did so now. He knew it was later, but his body didn't.

Both men arrived a little early.

"What have you got for me, Jack?"

"Hey, Tim. I don't think this will be anything complicated. This is concerning the home invasion and murder we had a couple of weeks ago. I don't really expect to find anything on the computer or on these disks," he said pointing to the stack of discs taken from Slaton's house. "But I am really anxious to look at what is on this one," he held up the baggie containing the single disc found in Slaton's car.

"Well, since that's the one that has your panties in a wad, we will look at it first."

Detective Smith snickered at Wilson's remark, and even Jack smiled. Wilson took a couple of minutes to hook up the computer and turned it on. He inserted the disk Jack gave to him and revealed its contents on the screen. Nothing. It was a blank disc. The two detectives were obviously disappointed, and just sat looking at the screen.

"Sorry, guys. Nothing here. Maybe what you are looking for is on one of the others."

Jack sighed, "Okay, let's look and see." He was not very hopeful.

It did not take long to look through the discs. Most were software drivers that had come with the computer. The others were all school related. It really was Greg Slaton's computer.

It was almost five when the two detectives went in to see Chief Pollock and report on the search results.

"What have you got?" he asked expectantly.

"A big zero, Chief. We don't have squat." Jack told him all the details of the search, what they found and where and what was on the discs. "And when I called to check on the money, the head of the finance and accounting department told me he did not know whether the president had given Slaton a bonus or not. He has given bonuses in the past and told him about it after the fact so they could keep the books in order. He couldn't ask Mr. Wooten about it because he was on a plane headed out of the country with, get this, the Vice-President of the United States."

"So all you have is some lock picking tools and a magnet, both of which Slaton has a ready explanation for, and money from an unknown source that may be perfectly legitimate. That and suspicions about three bullet holes that are close together. Is that right?"

Jack nodded glumly. "Yes sir, that about sums it up."

"Ya'll go home. You've been putting in a lot of overtime. Maybe you'll have a better day tomorrow. You are back to square one. Time to start over."

The men filed out, and said goodbyes, and then each went his own way.

It was after six when Jack got back to his place. He thought about going for a swim, since it was such a hot day, but the light breakfast he had eaten at eleven had totally worn off, and he was famished. He called Debra, who answered the phone on the second ring.

"Hey, I'm sorry I did not call you last night, but I did not get in until after one. We served that search warrant yesterday afternoon, and those things just take forever. I know it is late to be asking, but I just got in and I'm starving. Would you like to go down to the Gathering Spot with me and get a burger?"

"I was just fixing a sandwich, but that sounds better. I'll just drive over. See you in a few minutes."

Debra arrived, and the two walked down to the small restaurant on the apartment property and placed their order. There were several others there, eating or having a beer, and one couple was playing pool on the pay-to- play pool table. The television behind the bar was tuned in to NewsNow, and they watched Mia Munson and her two co-workers report the local news while they waited for their food. When it was ready, they took their plates over to a small table where they could talk.

"Were you calling about something specific last night or just to talk?" Jack asked

"Well, I was calling because of something I found out at work that really got to me, but now I think I was just letting my imagination get away with me."

Jack looked at her quizzically. "What is it?"

"Well, I went to eat lunch with Mary Hightower. She's Mr. Bolin's secretary, whom I've talked about. While we were out, I remembered that you wanted to know about a medical conference in Hong Kong, so I asked her if one was coming up that she knew about. She said no, because they just had one there a few months ago. Mr. Windom, the man who was killed, was scheduled to go, but at the last minute Mr. Bolin went instead."

Jack quit eating. "That's strange. He told me he didn't know anything about it. Why would he lie?"

"If I remember right, Jack, you asked him about a SARS conference, not a medical conference, so he didn't really lie He just did not tell you everything he knew. Maybe he just didn't think about it. You were asking about SARS, after all."

"Maybe, but I got the feeling when I was talking to him that he wasn't telling me everything. I think he thought about it and chose not to tell me. I wonder why. But what was it that freaked you out?"

"Jack, it is just too bizarre to think about, let's just forget it."

"Debra, I know you well enough to know that you don't get upset that easily. Tell me about it, you have my curiosity up now."

"After Mary told me that Mr. Bolin had gone to Hong Kong, and when he'd gone, I got to thinking about Cold-X. I have been reading the weekly progress report so I could know where we are on the project, and how we got there. The project report is like a diary that tells everything that has happened with the research. It tells about all the failures, the successes, the problems - everything. Anyway, I thought I remembered one observation that I read about half way through the report. I went back and looked it up again, and I was right. I can't tell you word for word, but basically it said that balium took control of the cold and then Cold-X killed the balium and the cold. So, the cure is a two-part deal, in the same capsule. But what it said that caught my attention was that if left alone, balium would intensify the symptoms of the cold and make them much stronger, even to the point that patients could die. It would also make the cold extremely contagious. I was thinking about the note that said balium equals SARS, and the medical conference...."

For the first time since she had known him, Debra heard Jack curse.

-42-

Tim Murray saw Bill Horton in the hall after lunch, and Horton motioned him into his office. "Did you see Mr. Wooten this morning?" Horton asked.

"No, was he here? I thought he was going to Washington."

"He has now, but he was here this morning. This thing with Windom is getting scary. The cops searched Slaton's house last night. It seems they think he did it. And maybe with good reason." He told Tim about the money, the disc they found in Slaton's car, and what Wooten's instructions were.

"So it was Slaton, huh? I should have figured. Is he at work?"

"Yes, they haven't arrested him, yet. Maybe, they won't. Mr. Wooten thinks there is an even chance they don't have anything at all. It all boils down to the disc. He figures that if they had anything else, they would have arrested him already."

"Yeah, well that doesn't give me a whole lot of comfort. He also thought we had already seen the last of the detectives, remember? Besides, they must have something to make them look at Slaton in the first place. Well, there is nothing that we can do. That is for sure. I'll see you. Let me know if you hear anything."

Tim went directly to Greg Bolin's office and told him everything. Bolin was at his desk, a stack of progress reports in front of him. He swore quietly.

"Damn, Tim, it feels like everything is falling apart. What are we supposed to do if they arrest Slaton? Wooten's already out of the country, which is where I would like to be right now. I've got a real bad feeling about all this. Don't you?"

"Yeah, I'm not real happy, either. But I don't know what we can do but ride it out. I'm sure that Wooten did not tell Slaton the real reason he wanted Windom out of the way. So, if they arrest Slaton, it would still take a lot to figure out the motive." He motioned towards the television where the latest development about SARS was being reported, complete with pictures of hundreds of Chinese citizens hurrying about with white surgical masks covering the bottom part of their faces.

Bolin watched the screen for a moment. "Jesus, Tim. I did not realize how devastating this would get. Mr. Wooten did. He even told us. I just didn't picture all of this. I know we decided the price was worth the result, but now I don't know."

"Wait a minute, Greg. Don't even go there. It's too late now. What's done is done. We sure as hell can't change it. We have enough problems right now. Don't start second guessing what we've done so far. We are on the home stretch as far as that goes. It won't be long before SARS is over, and people the world over will have a cure for their colds, and we will be making a fortune. Keep the big picture in mind. I know it is easy to look back and wish things were different when it gets tough going, but don't. Wooten's too powerful, and the cure is too important. We may have some tough days in front of us, but it will eventually work out."

"I know. Don't worry. I understand exactly where we are, and how we got here. I have no illusions about being able to change any of it. I'm not about to do anything to rock the boat. I'm just not as sure as you are that Wooten has things under control. I hope he does, and I hope you are right about his power and the cure being so important. Because that Detective Nebra is smarter and more tenacious than Wooten thought. He just keeps showing up. And you know that if Slaton breaks and Windom's murder is tied back to here, the next question will be why. What did he know? What was he working on? What could he have done to cause his murder? I might not like where we are right now, Tim, but believe me, I understand exactly where we are and what the risks are, and I'm not going to hide my head in the sand and get blindsided."

"Easy, Greg, I did not mean to upset you. I just felt like you were getting a little too remorseful for a minute, and we cannot afford that. Sorry."

Greg sat back in his chair. "No, you are right. I did not mean to unload on you. I know I can count on you, and I just wanted you to know that I still know what is going on. We have to count on Wooten, like it or not. I do worry about that bean counter, Horton, though. He is a weasel, and I just don't like him. But there isn't anything we can do now but see how it plays out. I've got to go to a staff meeting. We should be done by noon. Why don't we go play some racquetball at lunch? I feel the need for exercise."

"Sure. I could use a little release myself. I'll be in my office catching up on paperwork. Come get me after your meeting. And don't worry too much about Horton. He may be a weasel, but he's too involved to cause a problem. Remember the paper we all signed."

"Yeah, I haven't forgotten. I also haven't forgotten that the only person who has a copy of those is Wooten." He stood and the two men shook hands, more as a method of reassuring each other, than as good-bye.

Tim left, and Greg sat at his desk for a few more minutes, thinking. He knew that if this thing blew up, and they were found out, he would take the biggest fall. It was he who had unleashed the sickness that balium caused, as Wooten had so eloquently reminded him. He looked at the progress report on his desk. He had a staff meeting in ten minutes to discuss the latest developments in all of the projects his section was working on. He was not looking forward to it. The meeting would be the first for the group since Windom's death, and he knew there would be some discussion and questions about it.

Knowing what he now knew would make it tough. He felt queasy, being in such emotional turmoil. He had started the SARS epidemic, using the drug his researchers had developed as a *cure* for sickness - not a *cause*. Because he had done that, a member of their group had been murdered, and the company to which they had all dedicated themselves was in danger of collapse, if all were known. He had worked with these people for years and had earned their respect and allegiance. It had all seemed such a good idea at the time. He shook his head and reluctantly walked to the conference room for his meeting.

-43-

Jack apologized for his language, but could do nothing to temper his excitement. "That's it, Debra. You have figured it out!" he exclaimed. He jumped up and kissed her, right there in front of God and everybody.

"No, no, no, Jack. I'm not sure I have. I mean I had suspicions and was going over the project report trying to put it all together, but then I talked to Mr. Bolin this afternoon, and he is just so nice and laid back. There was absolutely nothing suspicious about the man. If he were guilty of this, there is no way he could act like that. I just cannot believe he would do something like that."

"You mean you don't want to believe it. I don't want to think that someone would intentionally cause all of those deaths and that devastation either. And you are right, Bolin has been a little nervous sometimes, but he never acted in a way that caused me to seriously suspect him of wrongdoing. But everything sure fits into place, doesn't it? And this would explain why Windom had to die. He figured out the same thing you did. And there would only be two places for him to go, other than the police - his supervisor, Bolin, or the president, Jim Wooten. Since he did not go to the authorities, he must have gone to one of them. I wonder how he did it. Did he threaten to expose them? Did he try to blackmail them? That could explain it, Debra."

"Well, just because it explains everything, doesn't mean there isn't another explanation, too. Remember, I've only been there a little while. I don't pretend to know all there is about it. I've just read the progress report. I wasn't involved in any of the research, and I could have missed something or not totally understood what I was reading. This research is very detailed and intricate; I could very easily be misunderstanding part of it. And if I am wrong, then that kills your blackmail theory - and you are right back to a random home invasion."

"Well, then, let's get it and go over it together. Maybe we can get some experts to look at it."

"I can't do that Jack. That is proprietary information, and I am sworn to keep it secret. I probably shouldn't have told you as much as I did, but I had too, and I did not divulge anything about the formula or tests or anything. They could not only fire me, they could put me in jail for theft if I were to bring that report out of the research area. Besides, I don't even have it any longer. Mr. Bolin came and got it this afternoon. It'll take a court order to get it, and you know they will fight you on that."

Jack leaned back in his chair. He knew she was right. He would talk to the DA tomorrow, and find out what they could do. They finished their meal in silence. Debra could tell that

Jack was worrying about the situation, and she was too. She was now involved in the investigation of a man she had never known, and whose death was now touching her business and private life. Even worse, she was working for a company that might be responsible for the deadly epidemic known as SARS. She felt very far removed from her first day at work, when she was so enamored with the company. Once she had felt very fortunate to have landed the job at Condor. Now, she somehow felt dirty. The work she had looked so forward to now looked tainted.

Jack paid for their burgers, and they started walking back to Jack's apartment, hand in hand, when Debra spoke. "Jack, this is the craziest mess I have ever seen. I don't know whether to be proud or disgusted about where I work. The people there are pleasant, helpful and professional, and I know they are dedicated to their jobs and are truly excited about the idea of finding cures for diseases and sicknesses. They work long hours, are always optimistic, and cherish every positive result of their work. It is a good company. But then when I think about Mr. Bolin and the possibilities the project report suggest about SARS, I get disgusted. How can something that evil be in the same environment? I just don't get it. It does not seem right."

"I understand what you mean, Debra. But I have seen it so many times. A person with a great job steals from his employer because he wants more. A mother, who by all accounts is devoted to her children and a model parent, goes out drinking and leaves them home alone to perish in a fire caused by the children playing with matches. A pro athlete with millions of dollars in endorsements and a beautiful wife gets caught with a prostitute or doing drugs or steroids and just loses it all. It doesn't compute, because it is stupid; it's greedy; it is self-indulgent; and it goes against our sensibilities. But it happens so often." He squeezed her hand and then half-joked, "Ya'll ought to be looking for a pill that would cure stupidity and greed, the demand is enormous."

Debra smiled appreciatively at his humor. "I know you are right. I read about things like that in the papers, but this is the first time I have experienced something like this first hand. And I'm still not positive I am now."

"Let's try to forget about it for a while. I want some experts to look at that project report, but I don't know how. Debra, for God's sake, please be careful at work. Don't let on you suspect anything is wrong." He put his arm around her and gave her a reassuring hug. "For now, let's do something else. Do you want to see a movie?"

-44-

Jim Wooten, Vice-President Nate McCoy, and Chinese ambassador Chong Ming arrived in Hong Kong in the early afternoon. They had an uneventful flight with good food and an open bar. They slept well on the plane and, after checking in to the hotel, Wooten felt rested and excited. He had been unprepared for the sight of so many people wearing surgical masks, even though he had watched them many times on the television news. He wanted to wander the streets and take in the sights, but because the Vice President was along, security was very tight, and they could not go anywhere alone.

The group planned to meet at five and go out for the evening meal and some entertainment. He was not looking forward to going, but knew he had to. He did not enjoy the company of the Vice-President, who he thought was an idiot. The Chinese ambassador was more likable; they just had nothing in common. And there was so much security, he felt like he was in a fish bowl. What he really wanted was a thick steak and a whole bottle of Crown Royal. He tried turning on the television, but could not understand anything that was being said. Oh well.

He pulled out his travel flask and poured a stiff drink, then sat down and tried to read the book one of the security officers had given him. It was a book about political corruption. Fitting.

The group went to an elegant, well-appointed restaurant where they were ushered into a private dining room. The room was extravagantly furnished with heavy red silk curtains, numerous oil paintings, ornate pewter ceiling tiles, hand carved furniture and a large Buddha.

They were met at the restaurant by the General Secretary of the Central Committee, one of the most powerful members of the Communist Party of China. His entourage of security, combined with those of the Vice President and the fanfare that accompanied them made for a very heady experience. The General Secretary spoke English and insisted on sitting next to Jim Wooten, a snub the Vice President chose to ignore. He interrogated Wooten at length about Cold-X and seemed satisfied and excited with the answers. His government had taken a lot of heat and ridicule over their handling of the SARS epidemic when it first started, and his country was still being decimated by the disease. They would gladly accept help from anyone, even the Americans. Perhaps this really would be a catalyst for normalized relations between the two countries. Jim was somewhat in awe of the power the man wielded and was delighted to bask in it for a while.

They enjoyed a five-course meal with plenty of Du Kang, a Chinese liquor. In fact, the Secretary General insisted Wooten's glass be refilled just about every time he took a sip.

As a result, the evening was far more pleasant than Wooten had anticipated. The Du Kang had a real kick to it, and Wooten realized he had better slow his consumption. They did not arrive back at their hotel until one in the morning, and by then, the jet lag was kicking in.

He showered and fell into bed immediately upon returning to his room. They were to meet for breakfast at nine and then go to the hospital. He slept soundly until seven thirty when security woke him. He felt groggy and a little washed out from too much alcohol and too little sleep, but the expectation of today's events, and three cups of strong coffee, soon revived him.

They were expected at the hospital and were treated as royalty. They met with a team of medical personnel in a room that could easily seat one hundred and was close to full. The ambassador, who was fluent in both languages, acted as interpreter.

The Vice-President spoke, "Ladies and gentlemen, it is with great pleasure that we are here today. Our countries have had differences and successes over the years. But in times of crisis, we come together not as Chinese or American, but as human beings, united for the good of mankind. With me today is Mr. Jim Wooten, who is president of the Condor Corporation, one of the United States premier pharmaceutical companies. He has brought with him a drug named Cold-X, which he says, and I believe, will cure the SARS virus."

There were mumblings throughout the room. Although this information had already been leaked to the attendees, this was a bold confirmation. He continued. "His company has been developing this drug for years as a cure for the cold, so it is not untested. Further, it has been tested on strains of the SARS virus, and has proven to be 100% effective."

There was applause and excitement throughout the room. The Vice-President continued for another ten minutes, boring everyone but himself. These people did not want to hear any more; they just wanted to see this miracle drug and put it to use.

Finally, he turned the microphone over to Wooten, who had a much better feel for the audience. He held up an oval yellow pill. "This is Cold-X. It works within 48 hours of ingestion. Let's go make some people well."

He got a standing ovation. The three men were taken to the intensive care unit by the hospital administrator and two doctors. Twelve patients, who were so sick the doctors had given up hope that they would live, were given the drug. One of the doctors turned to Wooten and the ambassador translated.

"If this drug works as you say, you will save many lives and probably this country. We will be forever in your debt. I am sure there will be a special place in heaven for you. Thank you." He had tears in his eyes.

Wooten smiled and thanked the doctor, and then the entourage left. He was feeling very good about himself. These people treated him with awe and respect, and he loved it. He never considered how they might treat him if they knew he wasn't really a savior. He was their worst enemy. They did not have a clue he had caused the disease that was devastating their country - a fact that Jim Windom found easy to forget, as well.

-45-

Jack arrived at work at seven in the morning. He had not slept well, and finally gave up about 5 o'clock. He went for an early morning jog, then showered and went to work. Detective Smith found him eating a donut and drinking his third cup of coffee when he came in.

"How can you eat like that and not gain weight?"

"I don't eat them much, and I already jogged this morning. Listen up, wait 'til you hear this." Jack told him about the conversation with Debra.

"Wow. That is some kind of serious. But what are we going to do about it. No way we are going to get a court order."

"I don't know. Let's get Chief Pollock and Daryl Warren, the DA, together and see what they suggest."

Smith nodded his agreement, and Jack picked up the phone and called the Chief and Daryl. They agreed to meet in Pollock's office at one. The Chief admonished Jack. "Don't be wasting our time. I don't know what could have changed since last night. You didn't have squat when you left here. This better be good."

Jack assured him it was and tried to concentrate on other tasks until their meeting. He and Smith went to Millie's, a popular lunch spot. Smith ate heartily, enjoying his chicken potpie and half of Jack's meatloaf.

They arrived at the Chief's office five minutes early and waited in the outer office until Daryl Warren arrived. The chief knew better than to keep Warren waiting, and they were ushered right in.

"Okay, Jack," Chief Pollack said, "talk to us. What have you got?"

Jack looked at the DA and brought him up to speed on the no results search warrant. He told them about Debra and her job, the weekly progress report, the scrap of paper from Windom's apartment, and then he told them about the medical conference. The men listened intently until Jack was finished. Then Chief Pollock spoke.

"So, what you are saying is that this Bolin guy, your girlfriend's boss, goes to Hong Kong for a medical conference, and while he is there, he spreads this balium around and starts the SARS epidemic. Then Windom finds out about it, and Bolin hires Slaton to kill him. But you don't have any evidence to support any of it, a motive or anything. The only evidence you know about, that might, and I emphasize might, give some support to it is protected information in a progress report that you can't get without a court order. And you would have to fight a major corporation to get that. A major corporation whose president is traveling with the Vice-President of the United States as we speak. Is that it?"

Fatal Healing

"No, sir, not quite. The motive part bothered me, too. I told you that Debra just started with Condor. Well, when they were giving her a little orientation, they told her that Condor owns a subsidiary company that makes all of those surgical masks and personal air purifiers that you see the Chinese folk using now. We pulled up the stock history last night and Condor stock has skyrocketed in the last two months, because of the tremendous sales volume and increased profits. Plus, Debra says that because of FDA rules and regulations it can take years for a drug to get to the market. Even though Cold-X is ready right now, it would not be approved for another two years. But if it is used to cure SARS, all of that might change. So the motive is money. You are right about the evidence though. That is why I wanted to meet with ya'll. I need suggestions. If I am right about this, we are not talking about one murder. We are talking about all of those SARS victims too."

Daryl Warren answered. "Jack, you are trying to climb Mount Everest, and you don't have any equipment for it. I'm not saying that you are wrong, as far-fetched as it might be, but you don't have any proof. There isn't a judge anywhere who is going to let you go on a fishing expedition at Condor, unless you have something pretty damn concrete for them to hang their hat on. I trust your instincts, but they aren't enough. And I honestly don't know what else to tell you. Get us some more proof."

The men all got up to leave. Jack and Joel were clearly dejected. Chief Pollock patted Jack on the shoulder.

"You are a good detective Jack, but you need to step back and look at this again. Consider the possibility that you are wrong about all of this. Take a fresh look at it."

"Yes sir."

The two detectives went back to Jack's office and started from scratch. They looked at pictures of the crime scene, went over the coroner's report, went over all their notes, the background checks, everything. They discussed and dismissed different scenarios. In the end they had nothing but Jack's suspicions. He was certain that Slaton was the one who had killed Windom, but he could not prove it. If he could tie Slaton and, by association, Condor, to the killing, then he might start getting somewhere. But all he had was a blank computer disc.

The men finished their day and went home. Jack went to bed before ten. Once again his mind continued to wrestle with the problem while he slept. When he woke, he immediately started thinking about the blank disc. And then, it hit him. The disk might have information on it after all. He rushed to the office and found Smith already there.

"I'm feeling really stupid right now."

"What is it?"

"The disc, the one we got from Slaton's car. We didn't check one thing."

"It was blank, Jack."

"We did not check it for prints. If Windom's prints are on it…"

Both men jumped up and headed downstairs to the evidence room.

Fatal Healing

-46-

Debra had a rough day at work, because she could not quit thinking about the possibility her boss and her company might somehow be responsible for SARS. She tried to concentrate on her work, but her mind kept coming back to that possibility. She knew she could not continue this way, but she did not know what to do. At lunch, she told Doug Malcolm, her project manager, she was sick and went home. She spent a miserable afternoon. Her dad called her around seven, and she talked with him at length.

"Debra, I am a cop, and it is my duty to uphold the law. But, the law is not always right or good. History is filled with people that broke the law for the good of others. Where would we be if our founding fathers had not broken the law? Slavery was once legal, that didn't make it right. You have to follow your conscience, Debra. You will not be able to live with yourself if you do not do what is right, even if the law says you are wrong. You are a smart girl, and you will figure out what to do. I have confidence in you. I love you, kid. Now, why don't you go to bed early and try to forget about all of this for a while."

And she did.

She went to work the next day feeling much better, now that she knew what she was going to do. She just did not know how. Her project manager gave her a ton of work to do, and she spent the entire day trying to complete it, breaking only for a quick lunch that she had brought with her.

Mary Hightower brought her lunch to the break room, just as Debra sat down. She walked over to Debra's table where a large window provided a good view of Condor's landscaped grounds. "May I join you?"

Debra looked up. "Hey, Mary. Please do. I haven't seen you in a couple of days. How are you?"

Mary sat down across from Debra. "Oh, I'm fine. Greg has had me covered up with paper work so I've been stuck behind the desk. But I have gone to the restroom a few times so I looked in on you. I didn't say anything because you seemed engrossed in your work. How is it going? Do you feel like you are starting to be a part of the team?"

Debra hesitated. "I guess so. I mean, I understand what I am doing, and the people are all so wonderful, that's been a real pleasure." Her voice trailed off as she spoke.

Mary looked at her quizzically. "Is something wrong, Debra? When we went to lunch last time I could tell you were upset about something and you seem to be now, too. I hope it isn't anything that I have done."

Debra looked at the woman who had befriended her from day one, who reminded her of her own mother, and who had encouraged her to get re-involved in church. "Mary, please, you haven't been anything but great. And I am fine. I'm sorry if

I've acted funny. I've just got to work a few things out in my mind I guess. Tell me what you have been doing outside of work. Have you seen your children lately?"

Mary took the hint, and gladly answered Debra. "Actually, I have. They all came to eat with us this past Sunday afternoon. It was great. We bought a new pool table for the basement, and we had a great time playing that and visiting. And I'm going to be a grandmother again. My youngest..."

Mary scarcely touched her lunch she was so engrossed in her story. Debra was happy to be with the woman and enjoyed the escape. They talked for a good while and tarried over lunch longer than either had intended. Mary looked at her watch and then at Debra in surprise.

"Oh my goodness. I've been so busy talking that I have hardly eaten a thing. I've probably bored you to death with all this. I'm sorry Debra."

"You haven't bored me at all. I enjoyed every minute of it. You took my mind off things, and I needed that."

"You know, Debra, if something is bothering you, I can be a good listener, not that you could tell that by the way I have been talking, but I am. If you ever want to talk about what is bothering you, I'm here."

"Thanks Mary. But it is all so crazy. I just have to work this one out myself. But I do appreciate your offer. Maybe I'll take you up on it later."

"Okay, just so you know I'm here. Gosh, I've got to go. I've got to get some things together for Greg. Mr. Wooten's in China and called to ask him for some information. I'd hate for him to call back, and Greg not have it."

Debra stared at Mary. "Mr. Wooten's in China?"

"Yes. It's very exciting. They think that Cold-X might be able to help cure this SARS epidemic. Isn't that wonderful?"

Mary was rushing to finish her lunch and get back to her work and did not even notice Debra's expression. She told Debra good-bye and hurried out. Debra sat at her table another five minutes seemingly looking at the lush landscaping, but seeing none of it.

-47-

The computer disc yielded a partial print that could very well be Windom's. It was not enough of a print that an expert could swear it was his, but it had enough matches to be pretty conclusive. In any event, it was all he had, and Jack took it to the Chief, who was really not all that happy to see him this soon. He looked at the report and agreed that it was at least something.

"Okay, Jack, bring him in for questioning. You can hold him for seventy-two hours and hope you get something else. Right now you have the unexplained money and this partial print. You and I both know you can't get a conviction out of just those."

They picked Slaton up at lunch, without incident. Word quickly spread through the company that the police had arrested him, but only a very few knew what the arrest was about. Tim Murray had seen it happen, and he called Greg Bolin and Bill Horton. The receptionist had told Mary, who mentioned it to Debra while they were walking to their cars at the end of the day.

Murray, Horton and Bolin met in Murray's office. They were all frightened, especially Bolin. They talked at length, but no one had any suggestions about what they could do. They each felt like it would be just a matter of time until the whole thing crashed in on them. And Wooten was in Hong Kong. Murray called Wooten's secretary and left an urgent message for Wooten to call him if she heard from him. The three men parted, each with their own thoughts and fears. They all felt that life as they knew it was coming to an end.

Slaton called his wife and told her he had been arrested, and tried to convince her not to worry, without success. She was crying when she hung up. True to his word, and much to Jack's exasperation, he refused to answer any questions at all. He would not tell them if he had a lawyer; how old he was; if he was hungry or anything. He just sat there and looked at them.

♦♦♦

When Debra got home, she immediately called Jack and left him a message. Then she went for a jog to help clear her mind and to burn off some nervous energy. When she got back to her apartment, Jack was waiting for her. She was sweaty and flushed and a little embarrassed to be seen that way.

"I guess you called because you heard we arrested Slaton?"

"Yes. I want to hear all about it, and I have some news for you too. Come on in and make yourself at home. There is some tea in the refrigerator. I'm going to get a quick shower."

She went upstairs and came back down fifteen minutes later dressed in shorts and blouse, and towel drying her hair. She did not know how beautiful she looked to Jack.

"Okay, tell me," she said.

Jack had long ago given up any notion he would not discuss the case with Debra. Without her, he would be floundering in this investigation, and he knew it. He explained about the fingerprint, the arrest and Slaton's stonewalling.

"We really don't have much. If he doesn't open up, or if we don't get more evidence, he is going to walk. We'll just have to see what the next couple of days bring. I doubt he'll stay quiet long. What is your news?"

Debra took a deep breath. "I ate lunch with Mary Hightower today. Guess what? You know you told me that Mr. Wooten was traveling with the Vice President? They are in China. It seems they think Cold-X might help cure SARS. This is just all too coincidental. Jack, I cannot continue to work there with the suspicions I have. Those poor people, all ill or dead because of SARS. If I can do anything to prove or disprove it, I have to do it. I would have brought that report home if I could. But Mr. Bolin has it in his office, and I can't get to it. Unless I go at night, when no one is there. I can always say I am working late. Lord knows I have plenty to do."

Jack sat back in his chair and absorbed what Debra had told him. This theory was starting to take root, and he was suddenly frightened for Debra. If it were true, these people had already shown they had no regard for human life. They would not hesitate to kill Debra if they thought she could expose them.

"I can't let you do that. If we are right, these people have already killed, and they would not hesitate to kill you, too. If you got hurt, I would never forgive myself. Come on. Let's go get something to eat and talk about this. We will go back to that Thai restaurant, how about it?"

Debra agreed and went back upstairs to finish drying her hair and to change clothes. She felt much better now for some reason. She had a plan and at least she had decided on a course of action. Despite Jack's protests, she was going to get that report. That was much better than wondering and fretting. She put on a little make up and went back downstairs. Jack got up from his chair and Debra was reminded again that he was an extraordinarily handsome man. But that was not all. He was a good and trustworthy man, and he was rapidly endearing himself to her. She briefly thought about how her life was a paradox. She was so happy about part of it and so frightened and dismayed about the other. Jack gave her a hug, sharing many of the same thoughts. Debra was an extraordinary woman, and he did not want to think about the danger she was in. They took her Miata, top down, to the restaurant.

They were seated in a small booth near the window. The waitress brought them water and took their order. After the waitress left, Debra put her hand over Jack's. "Jack, there is a saying about all is lost when good people sit by and do nothing. I can't do that. I have to do what is right. It is not just for you, it's for me, too. I have to live with the person I see in the mirror everyday. You need that report, and I need to get it for you. I'm going tonight."

Jack pleaded with her to wait a few days to see if he could find with another way, but she would not listen. Finally, he acquiesced. "Okay. But I'm coming with you."

-48-

Wooten and his entourage received news there were signs of improvement on all twelve patients about thirty-six hours after the first patient was administered the drug. It was the first improvement any had shown, and the doctor's and families were elated. By the time forty-eight hours had elapsed, all twelve patients were deemed well enough to be removed from the Intensive Care Unit. The Chinese ambassador was beside himself with delight, and the news media was starting to hear of the first real breakthrough in this disease that had devastated the country. They met with the hospital staff, and Wooten turned over the remainder of the samples he had with him to the very admiring and thankful doctors.

The Vice-President gave a ten-minute speech to the hospital administrators and a select group of the media, in which he managed to say absolutely nothing except the United States was proud and humbled to be able to help China during this time of internal turmoil. Everyone talked of being cautiously optimistic. More proof was needed before announcing a cure, but the process was underway.

The media had covered the Vice President's visit and speculation was rampant among them. But, there was no official announcement, and they dared not print too much without governmental approval. The government, already burned by their initial suppression of the SARS epidemic, took a wait and be certain attitude.

The ambassador was going to stay behind for a few weeks, and it was just Wooten and Vice President McCoy who boarded the plane for the long flight home. Both Vice President McCoy and Windom had been in periodic touch with the White House and specifically, Doug Champion. Those in the know were very excited, and White House personnel were gearing up for an extensive media blitz starting in the next several weeks. The world would soon know the United States and The Condor Corporation had stepped up to the plate and saved the day for China, for Canada, and for people everywhere.

Vice President McCoy had met with the General Secretary for several hours prior to the departure and returned from the meeting jubilant. After the plane took off, he shared with Jack, "The General Secretary said to tell you 'thank you,' and that he enjoyed meeting and talking with you. He is obviously very pleased with the results of your drug. They want to be sure there aren't relapses, or any side affects that show up later, but they are very confident now. Jim, I can't tell you how much this will ultimately mean to the United States. Of course curing this SARS epidemic is extremely important and will save many lives, but diplomatically, this is turning out to be the catalyst for normalizing relations between our countries. And I have no doubt it will improve our image globally, as well. I cannot tell you how important that is for our economy. I want to tell you personally that I am grateful."

Coming from the Vice President of the United States, this was pretty high praise, and Jim Wooten smiled cheerfully. "Thank you, sir. I wish I could take all the credit, but I can't. The research and development staff at Condor deserves that. And you can be sure that if all this works out the way it seems it will, they are in for a nice bonus."

"Yes, I expect so. It is important to keep good folks around and happy, right?"

"Exactly."

They two men talked for hours, something they had not done on the flight over or during their stay. Windom learned that McCoy was an avid hunter and had grown up in Montana, where his family owned a huge farm. According to the Vice President, it was God's country. The hunting was excellent, and the fishing was superb. The air was clean, and the sky was so clear you felt like you could reach out and touch the stars.

"Jack, last season, I was hunting pheasant with a group of eight other guys, and the first day we all bagged our limit of birds. I shot the biggest, prettiest rooster you have ever seen. I had to have it mounted. The taxidermist did a wonderful job. He mounted it as if it was in flight and I put it above the fireplace mantel. I will plan to have you out for a hunting trip next season, and you'll see it then. Do you think you can make a trip?"

"You, bet. I've been hunting all over the world, but somehow I missed Montana. I would love to come. You just let me know when, and I will be there."

They talked for a while longer, then the Vice President decided to lay down and get some sleep. Jim watched a movie and thought about the events of the past week. He was very content with himself. He had been treated like royalty in China, and everything was going according to plan. He had become accustomed to seeing people walking around with their surgical masks on, like it was part of a uniform or something. They would be able to forget the masks soon, but he was glad they bought them. It had really helped his bottom line. He and the Vice President were now on a first name basis and were future hunting buddies. Doug Champion was ecstatic about the events and assured Jim that the President was as well. Politically, he was a made man.

He turned his thoughts to his company. Cold-X was sure to be approved soon, so he no longer had to worry about the financial future of Condor. He had wondered occasionally about Rex Slaton, but he was not overly concerned. Even if Slaton were arrested and convicted, there was no evidence to connect him to Wooten. Slaton had no proof the money came from him. He would live up to his agreement to look after Slaton's family, if that became necessary, and that would keep Slaton in line. Sure, it would be a situation he would have to deal with in some fashion, but it wasn't the end of the world. He could always find another person to head up security.

-49-

After their meal Jack and Debra drove back to her apartment. It had turned dark, and there was a little crispness in the air that made the ride in the convertible Miata invigorating. Debra parked in front of her apartment, and they went inside. Jack sat on the sofa, and Debra heated apple pie in the microwave for desert. They ate in silence, each contemplating what they were about to do. They both knew that for all intents and purposes, this would be the end of Debra's job. There was a possibility that she would even face criminal charges, and Jack would face dismissal too, since he would be assisting her in a criminal act. If the progress report confirmed their suspicions, they would probably escape unharmed in the ensuing publicity and arrests. If it did not, then they would surely be in for a rough road. Jack talked to her again about waiting to see if they could get the information another way.

"How, Jack? I would love to not have to do this, but I can't figure any other way to get the information you need. Without it, how can you find out for sure if these people are guilty?"

"Well, if Slaton talks, there is no telling where that will lead us, but he hasn't said a word so far. We have to release him tomorrow because we don't have enough to charge him with anything, so I guess that is a dead end."

"So you are pretty much dead in the water as far as other leads, right?"

"Yeah, I hate to admit it, but that is right."

"Jack, there is no need for you to go. You don't need to take that risk. I'll just go get it and come right back."

"Debra, I promised your dad I would look after you. He is a very big man. I don't want to be on his bad side. I'll come with you. I'm confident you are right in your analysis. Once we have the evidence, they won't be able to touch us," he said hopefully. "Let's go."

The gate guard recognized Debra's car and waved her through. She parked in a space near the building. Judging from the cars in the lot, it was not unusual for people to work overtime. A security guard who had taken over the receptionist's desk after normal business hours greeted her and Jack. He was watching a Braves game on a miniature television, and gave Jack a visitor's pass without comment after he had signed in and shown identification. Jack had seen the pass card that enabled the elevator on his previous visits and was not surprised when Debra used hers. They got off at the third floor and passed the conference room. This was as far as Jack had ever been, and he was not prepared for the retina scan that Debra submitted to in order for the doors to the research area to open.

"They really are security conscious here. I have heard of those, but I've never seen anything like that," he commented softly.

"Yes, they are." Debra whispered back.

"Why are we whispering?"

Debra laughed nervously. "I don't know." She said in a normal voice. "It's just weird being the only ones here. Normally there are people everywhere."

They passed the area where she worked, and she pointed her desk out to Jack. "Right now, that is my desk. I probably won't ever see it again after tonight."

"We don't have to do this, Debra."

"I have to Jack. I have to."

They walked down the hall and entered the area where Mary Hightower's desk and the door to Mr. Bolin's office were located. Debra walked past the desk without hesitation and tried to open the door. Locked. She had not thought about that. Jack took out a credit card and tried to by-pass the lock, while Debra looked in Mary's desk for a key. She felt badly doing so. This was her friend's desk, and Debra felt like she was betraying her in some way.

◆◆◆

Greg Bolin's day had not been pleasant. When he heard of Slaton's arrest, he had felt physically sick. He did not have a family like Murray did, and for that, he was grateful. At least he only had to worry about himself. He felt like it was only a matter of time before everything blew up around them. Slaton would talk and incriminate Wooten. The ensuing investigation would reveal everything. He had counted up his available cash and wondered about fleeing, but there wasn't enough money to make that an option. He thought of just going to his houseboat on Lake Lanier and waiting for them to come for him, but that didn't seem appealing either. He was a smart man, used to success and used to things going his way. He sat at home and nursed a beer while he thought about his plight.

He knew that of the four, he was especially vulnerable. He was the one who had gone to China and started the SARS epidemic, and it would be him that everyone was after. He pictured the headlines and himself in handcuffs. How had it come to this? Six months earlier, he had been a successful, sought-after bachelor with the world at his feet. He could afford to go anywhere and do anything. Now, he pictured his life in ruins.

The research for Cold-X was contained in thousands of volumes of papers, and given time, the cops would figure it all out. But there was only one place that everything was summarized for them, he thought now. The weekly progress reports. He left his home and headed for the office. If he was going down, he wasn't going to make it easy for them.

As Jack tried to open the door to Bolin's office with his credit card, and Debra searched Mary's desk for a key, Greg Bolin was parking his car in his reserved space. He did not notice Debra's car parked just a few rows away. He stopped off at the men's room in the lobby and then got on the elevator and started for his office.

-50-

Police Chief Raines sat in his Sylvester Georgia home and flipped through the channels on the television, seeing nothing. His mind was over a hundred miles away, worrying about his daughter. She had been very troubled when he talked to her last, and he had done his best to help her. He really wasn't sure what he should do. He wanted to just go to Atlanta and get her, bring her home and protect her. But he knew he could not, that she would not come. She was an adult now and was making it on her own. He was as proud of her as he was worried about her. He offered a silent prayer to God to keep her safe and to give her courage and wisdom to do the things she needed to do. He prayed to God, but his faith was in Jack Nebra right now. Jack had promised to look after Debra, and Chief Raines was depending on it. He would not be at all happy if he knew where they were, and what Debra and Jack were doing now.

♦♦♦

The key was under the calendar, right on top of the desk. Jack had only managed to mangle his credit card, and it was now unusable. They entered the office and shut the door behind them. The light from the parking lot shined through the window, illuminating the room just enough for them to see. Deborah went to the bookcase from which she had seen Mr. Bolin take the progress report. The report was on the end of the second row, and she found it easily. She opened it up to make sure it was what they were looking for. Jack was looking over her shoulder.

They were both startled when the lights came on and whirled in unison to see who had entered the office. They faced Greg Bolin, who stood, keys in hand and mouth open, taking in the scene of his new research assistant and the police detective looking at the very report he had come to destroy.

His face drained of color, and he cursed and ran from the room. Jack and Debra ran after him. They did not know whether he was going for the security guard or what, but they knew nothing good would come from them staying where they were. Bolin had a head start, and the elevator was still on the third floor when he got to it. Jack and Debra had to wait on the second elevator to arrive. Debra clutched the progress report tightly to her chest.

"What now?" she asked.

"I don't know. I don't know if he is running from us, or to someone. But we have to get out of here with that book. Otherwise, you just blew a good job for nothing. If the guards try and stop us, you go for the car, and I'll stay here and try to control things."

They reached the first floor and saw the security guard standing up behind the receptionist desk, staring at the door closing behind Bolin. He was not used to seeing people run out of the building that way. Jack and Debra ran past him, too, and he quickly talked into his radio. Something was wrong, but he did not know what it was.

Bolin jumped into his Jaguar and squealed his tires, leaving the parking lot. Jack took Debra's keys from her and quickly followed after him. The guard stood outside the guardhouse and looked in amazement at the shattered arm of the gate. Bolin had not even slowed down as he went through. Jack reacted from instinct. He did not know where Bolin was going, but he knew the actions of a guilty man. Bolin was running, and that made Jack want to catch him. Debra did not know her car could go so fast so quickly. Still, it was no match for Bolin's powerful Jaguar.

Bolin was panicked, and he knew it. He tried to calm down, but he knew all was lost. His worst nightmare was confirmed in the white light of his office, when he saw Debra and Detective Nebra looking at the progress report. He could not believe he had been so stupid. He should never have let her see the report; that project was damn near done anyway. Why had he bothered to let her get involved in it? He was traveling close to one hundred miles an hour when the deer stepped into the road and stopped, blinded by the headlights. Bolin swerved and lost control. The Jaguar hit the bridge railing coming to a screeching halt. Bolin did not. He was dead when he hit the ground far away from his smoking car.

Jack and Debra arrived at the scene a few minutes later. Debra sat in shock at the turn of events, while Jack used his cell phone to call 911. Debra could see the smoking remains of the Jaguar and the smashed bridge railing. She got out of her car and ran to where Jack stood. The windshield of the car was gone. She could see Bolin's crumpled body far down the embankment. Jack ran to the man, but Debra did not. She knew he had to be dead. She leaned against the crumpled car and waited. She could hear sirens in the distance and soon the scene was bathed with the bright search lights of two police vehicles. An emergency response team arrived, and she watched them load Bolin onto a stretcher and cover his body with a sheet.

Debra watched as they put her former boss in the back of the ambulance and leave without sirens or lights. There was no reason for them to rush. She felt terribly sad and completely washed out. He had seemed such a fine, brilliant person. Now he was gone, and Debra was sure the progress report would ultimately prove he really was not such a fine person after all. Jack put his arm around her and led her to her car. He knew it was going to be a very long night.

-51-

Wooten was anxious to get back home. They arrived in Washington close to midnight, and he had walked over to the Delta counter and managed to get on the red eye flight back to Atlanta, which left at one in the morning. It was after four when he got home. He slept until eleven, ate some cereal and took a cab to Tara Field Airport where he retrieved his car and drove to his office. He saw the board was broken off the guard gate and wondered what that was about. He accepted a stack of messages from his secretary, including the one marked urgent from Tim Murray. He returned that call first and Murray picked up immediately. There were no pleasantries.

"Have you heard the news?"

"No, I just got in a little while ago. What is it?"

"They arrested Rex Slaton day before yesterday."

"Have you talked to the police to find out what the charges are or anything?"

"No."

"Well, as Vice President of Personnel, maybe that would be a good idea. Why don't you do that and call me back."

Tim Murray took Nebra's card from his wallet and called his number. "Detective Nebra, this is Tim Murray, over at Condor Corporation. I met you in Rex Slaton's office a couple of weeks ago. I understand that ya'll picked up him up. What is he charged with?"

"We have not officially charged him yet, but we expect to charge him with the murder of Gene Windom."

"You have to be kidding. What possible motive would he have to do that?"

"Mr. Murray, we don't know yet what all is going on over at Condor, but we expect to know soon. Rex Slaton isn't Condor's only problem. Greg Bolin was killed in a car crash last night while he was speeding away from Condor. He is the one who crashed through your gate arm. Right now, the District Attorney is looking over a progress report on the drug Cold-X."

He heard a sharp intake of breath from the other end and Murray said, "Oh, my God."

"Like I said, we don't know what all is going on, but we will soon. If you have anything you need to tell us, I suggest you do it right away."

"I can't believe this. Greg Bolin, dead. I have to go. I'll call later."

A very shaken Tim Murray went to see Jim Wooten. Wooten's secretary took one look at his face and knew something was terribly wrong. He walked right past her and entered Wooten's office without knocking.

"Boss, Greg Bolin was killed in a car wreck last night. Nebra said he left here at a high rate of speed. He also said they have a copy of the weekly project report on Cold-X, and he indicated they think something is going on over here. Slaton is going to be charged with Windom's murder." He said all of this without taking a breath, and then flopped down into one of the chairs in front of the desk.

Wooten had just come in from his whirlwind trip to China, and was still high from the euphoria of his successes there. Everything was going exactly as he had hoped. He was not about to let this thing implode now. He stared at Murray for a moment, then picked up the phone and called his friend Russ Rawlings, who was a very prominent and influential attorney.

"Russ, I've got a real problem. Can you meet me at the Douglas County D.A.'s office right away?"

"Tell me what for, so I'll be prepared."

"I only know that I have one employee dead from gunshots, and another who is charged with killing him. I've got a third employee who was killed in a car crash last night, supposedly fleeing here, and now the cops have an internal document filled with extremely important proprietary information. I want it back."

"Jesus, Jim! Why couldn't you have something easy, like a DUI or something? This sounds pretty serious. Okay, I'll be there in thirty minutes."

Wooten looked at Murray. "It's not over yet," he growled.

Jim Wooten was not a man to trifle with, and the few who had tried in the past, did so to their own peril. No one tried to cross him twice. He was smart and could think on his feet. In addition he was wealthy and very powerful. He did not frighten easily, and he was at his best when the chips were down. He was going to need all of these attributes to survive this one, and he knew it.

He called George Champion on his cell phone as he drove to the courthouse.

"I'm surprised you aren't still asleep," George said when he answered.

"I wish I were, then maybe this would be just a bad dream. I've got a problem, George. I may need your help."

"What is it?"

"I'm not sure yet. But I should know shortly. All I can tell you is that one of my employees was killed in a car wreck fleeing Condor last night, and now the DA's office has a project report that details every aspect of Cold-X. I've got millions invested in that product and everything about it is spelled out in that report. Everything. Formulas, tests, everything. I'm on my way there now to get it back, I hope."

"It sounds like your employee was stealing your work. You probably won't have a problem, at least I hope not. We can't afford to have any bad press now. We are getting ready to have a major publicity push on this, as you know. Call me if you need me."

Wooten arrived early and was waiting in the outer office area when Russ Rawlings arrived. Daryl Warren was a very powerful man locally, but he knew better than to keep the president of the Condor Corporation and the metro area's most prominent attorney waiting, appointment or not. The men were ushered back to his office as soon as Rawlings arrived. The three men all shook hands and greeted each other.

"I assume you are here about this," Warren said indicating the three-ring notebook on his desk.

"Yes, that and a few other things," Wooten began. He stopped when Rawlings put his hand on his forearm.

"Jim, let's find out what's going on first. That book isn't going anywhere. Darryl, enlighten us. Who was killed, why, and what are you doing with that project report?"

"I'll be happy to tell you all I know. But I think it would be wise if we got Detective Nebra over here. You may have questions I can't answer, and he is the man on this case. Let me call him."

Detectives Nebra and Smith and Chief Pollock arrived within ten minutes and interrupted the DA in the middle of one of his yarns about his days as a Jag officer in the Navy. It was one of his favorite stories about almost getting left in port as his ship sailed off. He was running down the street, zipping his pants and carrying his shoes when they arrived. He was sorry he could not finish the story. Everyone stood up, and Warren made introductions all around. His secretary brought in two more chairs and everyone sat down.

"Jack, tell us everything you can about this thing. These guys are not our adversaries, and they have a right to know what is going on. Mr. Wooten here is a very busy man, and I don't want to waste his time. And I'm sure he has no desire to waste Mr. Rawling's time, since he's paying him.

Jack, who did not know for sure how far up the food chain this thing with SARS went, was reluctant to tell all he suspected. But he had no choice but to tell all he knew for fact. He started with the murder of Windom, and the things that led them to suspect Slaton. He told them about the scrap of paper found in Windom's apartment, and how Bolin had been less than forthcoming about the medical conference in Hong Kong. He told them Ms. Raines had put it together that SARS may have actually been caused by introducing balium into the Chinese population during the medical conference, and explained how they had gone to Condor last night to get the project report. He told them Bolin had come in, found them, and run, and he gave details about the fatal wreck. When he mentioned Debra's name, it was the first time that Wooten learned of her involvement, and everyone could tell he was none too happy about it. Debra had told Jack the night before that she was not going back to the Condor Corporation, and he knew that she could not. Talk about burning bridges... she had put dynamite under hers.

Russ Rawlings spoke when Jack was finished. "That is the most preposterous allegation that I have ever heard. You have absolutely no proof. You have taken the hallucinations of a young, newly hired employee, who is probably way over her head and totally stressed out, and concocted a story that is slanderous at best. You have imagined crimes where there are none. You have charged an employee with the one crime you do have, with evidence that would be thrown out of any court. Further, you intimidated and frightened another employee to the point he panicked and then died in a car crash. I think you

Fatal Healing

have a lot of explaining to do. In fact, I think that criminal charges are appropriate against Ms. Raines and you, Detective Nebra. Now, I suggest that you give us that stolen report immediately, and that you release Slaton without delay." He held out his hand for the report, but Pollock made no move to hand it over.

"I don't think so, counselor, not yet. I have looked at this report at length with Ms. Raines, and I think there is enough here to warrant a full investigation. If Detective Nebra is right, this is a crime of huge proportion, and I intend to make sure the proper authorities evaluate it. I'm sure the FDA and the FBI have plenty of qualified help and the resources to evaluate this report. Based on the information provided by Ms. Raines and the events of last night, I have prepared a subpoena for this document."

He nodded at Jack, who handed the attorney the subpoena.

"As far as Rex Slaton goes, you are right that we don't have enough evidence to charge him, yet. He was released a short while ago." He looked at Wooten. "I don't suppose you would like to comment on the money that Slaton came into?"

Rawlins answered for Wooten. "At this time, I am advising my client to answer no questions at all. As for this subpoena, I don't believe it will hold up when challenged. You know damn well that a subpoena comes before, not after you have the document. Further, gentlemen, that book represents millions of dollars in research and development. If the information contained in it falls into the hands of another pharmaceutical company, it would cause irreparable harm to my client."

"We will take good care of it," said Pollock.

There was nothing more to say and Wooten and his attorney left. Russ walked Wooten to his car. "Jim, could any of this be true about that chemical causing SARS?"

Wooten had been thinking about what his best response to this question would be. A back-up plan had been formulating in his mind, but he wasn't ready to give voice to it yet. He said simply, "I'm a business man, not a scientist, but I have no reason to believe any of that. I don't believe it is true. There is nothing to it."

-52-

Wooten drove back home. He had too much on his mind to go back to the office today, and the jet lag was kicking in. He was exhausted. He set the alarm to wake him up an hour later and fell instantly asleep. He woke somewhat refreshed and decided on a plan of action. He knew the secret was out, and the truth about SARS would be easily proven, now that authorities had a blueprint and knew what to look for. His only concern now was to protect himself and to salvage as much as he could.

He called George Champion, and they talked for quite a while. He basically told George that his top research scientist, a man he had personally recruited and in whom he had placed great trust, had betrayed him and his company. He did not have all the facts yet, but it appeared, for reasons only he could have answered, that Greg Bolin had gone to China during the medical conference and introduced balium into the population, causing the SARS epidemic. Evidently, the project manager, Gene Windom, had figured out what had happened, and Bolin killed him, too.

The President's Assistant Chief of Staff cursed long and hard. "Jim, this thing could totally backfire on us now. If China finds out that someone from the United States actually caused the epidemic, it will kill all possibility of good relations. It will give credence to all the bad things people have said about our country. We just cannot let that happen. I think you better get back to Washington as soon as you can. How quickly can you get here?"

"I'll call now. If I can charter a plane, I'll be there in a few hours."

"Call me back, and let me know. I'll pick you up at the airport."

They hung up and Wooten called Smith Air, a number he now knew by heart. They had a Falcon jet and pilot available. He packed a bag with enough clothes for three days and went to Tara Field airport. He would be in Washington by five. He sat back in his seat as the plane lifted from the ground and contemplated his reversal of fortune. Just yesterday his world was perfect, now it would take some very quick maneuvering for him to even stay out of jail.

George Champion picked him up at Reagan Field, and they drove to the Whitehouse. By six o'clock they were in a meeting with Lynn Means, Chief of Staff, and Joan Hadley from the FDA. George had warned him on the drive over, they were all upset about the situation, but Wooten was still unprepared for their greeting. They were talking when he was ushered into the conference room, but ceased when he entered.

Without any pleasantries Lynn Means said, "Sit down, Mr. Wooten, and tell us how in the hell you let this happen. Do not leave anything out and do not sugar coat it. We need to know the facts, and we need to know them now."

Jim sat down in a chair and looked around the room. He had never been to the White House before, and he had expected more. The room was painted white, and there were no pictures on the wall. The table was of good quality wood, but it had seen better days. The chairs were simple and dated. He had seen better furnishings in his doctor's office. He placed his hands on the table and looked at the grim faces on the two women.

"I did not 'let this happen,' anymore than you did. I cannot control what employees do of their own initiative. I will be glad to tell you anything that I know for fact, and I will tell you what I suspect. But I want you both to understand something. I am not guilty of a damn thing except trusting an employee when I should not have. If that is a crime, I am quite sure that everyone in this room has been guilty of it at some time or another.

Now, what I know is that Greg Bolin, who was the head of my research department, went to China for a medical convention. The police tell me he apparently took some balium - the agent in Cold-X that takes over the cold - with him, and somehow, introduced it into the population, causing the SARS epidemic. Now, I don't know how they arrived at this conclusion, or if it is correct or not. It seems that a new research assistant, a girl who has been with us for less than a month, found some information in a progress report that caused her to draw that conclusion about Bolin, and she stole the report and gave it to the police. Bolin walked into his office and found her and a detective taking the report, and ran, lending some credence to their story. I guess he was obviously guilty of something, or he would not have run; he would have had them held by our security force. While he was trying to get away, he lost control of his car, hit a bridge support and is now dead.

I also know that Greg's chief assistant was murdered in his home a few weeks ago, and it was that investigation which eventually led them to Condor. The detective investigating that murder is the same one who was in on stealing the report. If they are correct about Bolin starting SARS, then I suspect the research assistant who was killed found out about it, and Bolin killed him. The only reason I can come up with as to why Bolin did it, if he did it, is for money. He owned a lot of company stock and, quite frankly, when Cold –X is approved the value of that stock will be immense. I don't know if he was having money problems or what. He was a single guy, and he liked to gamble. Maybe he was in over his head and needed money quickly. I don't know. Maybe he figured out that when Cold-X cured SARS, the drug would quickly be put on the market."

"That is pretty convenient for you, isn't it?" asked Joan Hadley. "If this Bolin guy would become wealthy because of this, what about you?"

"Ms. Hadley, for your information, I am already wealthy. I do not owe anyone money, and I would have no problem waiting for the drug to be approved through normal channels. I came to Washington and told you all I knew about the drug because I felt it would kill SARS, and it was my duty as a human being to help end the epidemic, if I could. Greg Bolin headed up our research department, and it was he who brought me the test data that I shared with you. Now, I have told you what I know, and I will be happy to answer any questions you may have."

"Do you have any idea of the predicament this puts America in?" asked Lynn Means.

"I know it is a problem. I won't pretend to know all of the political nuances. But again, I did not cause this problem. It is my problem too. And quite frankly, it was not my idea for our government to use the SARS cure as a political cure as well. I simply came here because I had the drug and I wanted help in getting it approved and in use. Someone else gets credit for the political part of this mess."

The chief of staff sighed. "You are right about that, perhaps we should not have approached it the way we did. Hindsight and all that. Listen, we aren't going to accomplish any more tonight. I've still got to brief the President and some others. Can you be back here at nine tomorrow? George will take you to your hotel and pick you up in the morning, if that works for you."

"That is fine. I'll be here."

George Champion drove a thoughtful Wooten to the Watergate Hotel and bade him goodnight after making arrangements to pick him up at eight-thirty. Wooten checked in and had a drink in his room before going down to the hotel restaurant for supper and several more drinks. His mood was somber, and he reflected on his last trip to this town, when he was being treated warmly and everything was going his way. He did not know how all of this would turn out, but he had a few ideas that might help. Whether the powers-that-be liked it or not, they were joined at the hip with him. They could not afford to let him be destroyed. If they did, he certainly would not be silent about the government's involvement. He would scream it from the rooftops if he had to.

Fatal Healing

-53-

Word of Greg Bolin's death was received with dismay at the Condor Corporation. Tim Murray met with department heads and broke the news, after first going to the research department and telling that entire staff. He was sparse on details, telling them only that Greg had been killed in a single vehicle car wreck. It did not take long for more of the story to come out. They all had seen the broken security gate arm, and Mary Hightower was concerned because Debra had not shown up or called in. She knew from past experience, the security force here seemed to know everything, so she talked with Security Officer Billups, who told her that Tim Murray had left instructions to void Debra's security clearance because she was terminated. He also shared with her that Bolin had crashed through the gate and had been followed by Debra and Detective Nebra just before having the wreck that killed him.

Mary returned to the office and met Doug Malcolm, head of the heart stent research project and Debra's former project manger, on the elevator. He had just met with Tim Murray and gotten the word on Debra. The two went into Bolin's former office and compared notes.

"Officer Billups told me that Debra and Detective Nebra were here last night, and so was Greg. Something happened that caused Greg to tear out of here and crash through the guard gate. Jim said that Debra and the detective were right behind him, and that the wreck happened shortly after that. When I got here this morning, the door to this office was wide open. Greg never did that. He always locked it. When I tried to lock it back, I found that my key to it was gone. That's all I know. What did Mr. Murray tell you?"

"It was actually pretty weird. You know how he is always so friendly and interested in what you are doing. Well, he seemed very subdued and was not very forthcoming at all. He just told me that Debra Raines was no longer employed here and would not be back. He said that if she called or made any contact with us, we should notify him immediately. He did not offer any explanation, and made it pretty clear he did not want to discuss it. Then, Mr. Horton came in, and he looked like he was scared to death. I don't know what is going on, but I don't like it. First Gene Windom is murdered, and now Greg is dead and Debra's fired. Oh, when I left Murray's office, I could hear Mr. Horton asking him what they were going to do now. I don't know, Mary. Obviously, all is not as it should be. Let me know if you hear anything else."

Bill Horton was frightened and seemed on the verge of a nervous breakdown. "I tried to call Mr. Wooten, but his secretary said he was in Washington and could not be reached. Do you know anything about that? What does it mean?"

"I don't know Bill. I hope it means he has figured out a way to get us out of this mess. He called me just before he left for Washington and told me that was where he was headed, but did not say why. You know how he is; he plays it pretty close. He did tell me the police would not return the project report, because I asked him."

Horton looked even more frightened. "What project report?"

"You didn't know? That's what this is all about. Debra Raines and Detective Nebra took the project report on Cold-X. I guess Greg found them, panicked and ran. Mr. Wooten and some high powered lawyer went and met with the cops to try and get it back."

"No, I did not know all of that. If they have the report, we are finished, aren't we?"

"I don't know. I guess that is why Jim is in Washington. You know the government was pretty excited about Cold-X. I'm still betting on Jim. He is one smart s.o.b."

"I wish I could share that confidence. But I can't. Jim has been wrong about that detective the whole time. Every time we mentioned him, Jim would just dismiss our fears. I hope you are right, but I am not counting on it. But I know what I am going to do. I'm going home and get really drunk."

With that, Horton left. He was a sad, frightened little man, and Tim actually felt a little sorry for him. Tim sat behind his desk, contemplating his future. His wife knew that Bolin had been killed, and there was a real problem at work, and had sympathized the way she always did. She went shopping. His children, away at college, knew nothing, and he hoped he could keep it that way. He opened the drawer to his desk and removed the pistol he kept there. He checked the bullets out of habit, even though he knew it was loaded. He had over a million dollars in life insurance. He hoped it would not become necessary, but he had thought about it all night. Suicide was a better alternative than jail for him and financial ruin for his family. Also, he would never be able to bear the disappointment of his children. That would be more devastating to him than anything. He would wait and see what Jim Wooten was able to accomplish, but he would carry the gun with him at all times. If it came down to it, and he had time, he would make it look like and accident and just step in front of a bus or something. But if they tried to arrest him, he would be prepared. The gun was a small derringer and fit easily into his waistband and was hidden by his jacket. He continued to sit at his desk, thinking and accomplishing nothing.

-54-

Jim Wooten woke from a fitful sleep at six and staggered to the shower. He had drunk too much, had frightening dreams and slept badly. He felt much better after the shower and went down to the restaurant for breakfast. He knew he needed to fortify himself because today would arguably be the most important of his life. He was looking forward to today's meeting with a mixture of anticipation and dread. He had an idea, he just hoped it would work.

George Champion picked him up right on time, and, after a perfunctory greeting, they rode in silence until they were parking the car. As they got out of the vehicle, George finally spoke. "Jim, I guess we helped create this mess, and I sure wish we hadn't. There are a lot of folks that are running scared right now. You have always been a good contributor to us and I better warn you. The President is really ticked, and he is looking for someone to take the blame. Be careful in there."

Wooten nodded his head, and they entered the White House without speaking again. Today, they met in a larger, better appointed conference room. Present were Steve Presley of the Attorney General's office, Chief of Staff Lynn Means, Vice President Nate McCoy, several other people who remained unidentified, and a stenographer. They had obviously been waiting for Jim to arrive. They greeted him friendly, if not with warmth. The chair at one end of the table was the only one empty, and he took it.

Lynn Means spoke. "Jim, I have briefed these folks about our meeting last night. Mr. Presley has some questions that I hope will help resolve this problem." She nodded to Presley, who sat holding a pencil between his fingertips.

Wooten noticed the stenographer was taking down everything that was said and made a mental note to choose his words carefully. Now, he simply nodded his head and waited for the questions.

Presley began. "Mr. Wooten, as I understand it, you claim no knowledge of your associate's actions in starting the SARS epidemic. Is that right?"

"First off, calling him my associate is not accurate. He was an employee. And he may or may not be guilty of anything. I have not seen any evidence of it yet, but if he is, I had no knowledge of it."

"We have been in touch with the detectives on this case. That would be Detectives Nebra and Smith. You know them, correct?"

"Yes."

"They have a pretty convincing story, one that could be proven, I think. But, let's put that aside. Just to be sure I understand, and for the record, you claim no knowledge of any scheme to infect the Chinese population so that you could market your drug, is that a true statement?"

"Absolutely."

"You realize that our country is in a perilous position because of this, and as president of the company, you will be held accountable though, don't you?"

"Maybe. Maybe not. But blaming me is not going to help you, is it? In fact I think that is the last thing you want to do."

"Explain yourself."

"Look, I came to Washington because my company had a cure for SARS. If Greg did start it, I did not know about it. I came because I had the cure and I wanted assistance in providing it. It was not my idea to make this a big political deal, but I went along with it because it helped me, and because I want to benefit my country whenever possible. Now, if ya'll intend to burn me on this thing, you can be damn sure the American people and the Chinese people and the whole damn world will know the whole story." He sat back in his chair; he had not intended to be quite that blunt.

"Is that some kind of threat?"

"No, of course not. It is just fact. There is no way that I could go to any trial without the whole thing becoming public. And, last I heard, a person is still innocent in this country until proven guilty. That will mean a trial. But there is another way."

"What is that?"

"Look, let's not play games. You know what I am talking about, or you would not be here."

The meeting continued for another two hours. Wooten had given everything a lot of thought last night, and he knew he held enough cards to win. He was no longer intimidated. In fact, he was kind of enjoying himself. The questioning and sparring continued for only a short time. Now they just had to work out the mechanics of it all. They broke for lunch in the White House cafeteria, another first for Wooten, and afterwards, only Wooten and Presley returned to the conference room. The men talked and negotiated at length. When it was over, they stood and shook hands. Presley walked over to a phone on one of the coffee tables and made a phone call. A few minutes later the door opened, and George Champion walked in.

They left the White House before dark, and George drove him to the airport. His demeanor was better, and he smiled and clapped Jim on the back. "Have a good flight, Jim. We'll be in touch."

Fatal Healing

-55-

Two days later Jack Nebra received a phone call from his chief. "Ya'll better come up here, Jack. Daryl Warren is here, and he's got some news."

Jack and Detective Smith knew when they walked into the office that Chief Pollock and the DA were unhappy. Jack had never seen the normally outgoing and flamboyant DA so tired looking.

"It is all over, boys," the DA said. "National Security. I got a call from the White House this morning, and shortly after that, two FBI men showed up with a federal court order and took the project report. We have been ordered to drop all investigations into this affair for reasons of national security. That includes the investigation into the murder of Gene Windom. The story is that Greg Bolin killed him, and frankly, that may actually be the case. Now that Bolin is dead, too, there is nothing left to do. We are not to even speak about this case again. Everything you suspected may be true, but if it is, they got away with it. I am sorry. I know ya'll worked hard on this, and it really goes against the grain."

There was nothing left to say. Jack Nebra looked at Detective Smith and shrugged his shoulders. They both knew, and the other men in this room knew that justice was not well served in this case. They knew, but they could not prove it. And they were powerless to even try. Jack had a sour taste in his mouth, and for the first time in a long time, he felt like getting drunk. Instead, he left the room and went to the gym, where he took out his frustrations on a punching bag.

Later, he took Debra out to eat and broke the news to her. It was not a pleasant conversation. She had risked her life and sacrificed her job because she refused to stand by and let evil go unrevealed, and it was all for naught. He understood all too well. They discussed the case at length, and Jack tried to bring some closure.

He had gone over the events time and again, yet he knew that regardless of any action they might have taken, the results would have been the same. Condor was just too powerful and too well connected. He did not really understand all the political aspects, but he was smart enough to realize the United States could not afford to be seen as somehow responsible for the SARS epidemic. And he knew that world wide opinion would be damning if the story were known. But he could not help but remember the emotional distress of Windom's ex-wife, and their two children. He could not forget the horrible picture of thousands of people wearing surgical masks and living in fear of an invisible killer.

He had to reconcile himself to the fact that sometimes, those in power had to choose between horrible events.

Neither was desirable, so they chose the lesser of evils...he guessed.

Debra respected all that Jack told her, but she remained unconvinced.

Two months later

Debra Raines found another job, teaching high school chemistry, taking the place of a teacher who was pregnant. It did not pay nearly as well, but she enjoyed it. She would get by. When she let herself think about it, she would still get upset about the whole business with Condor. She had seen Mary Hightower at church, and they enjoyed a long talk. There had been a major shake up in the company. The Board of Directors had fired Jim Wooten, but had given him an enormous amount of money to leave. There were allegations of financial shenanigans and Tim Murray, who was now the acting president, had fired Bill Horton. Rex Slaton was still there as head of security, and he seemed to be doing fine. Everyone was just hoping things would get better.

Jack and Debra's relationship had continued to mature, and they were seeing each other exclusively. They shared many good times and had entered a comfortable stage in their relationship. The only real scar was that top people at Condor had totally gotten away with everything. It was just not right, and it gnawed at them both. They rarely spoke of that night when they had taken the progress report and Bolin had died, although Debra sometimes re-read the fifteen pertinent pages of the report that she had copied that night at the police station. It was while Jack and Debra were eating supper in his apartment and watching NewsNow that Debra first thought of it. She talked it over with Jack, who told her that he personally could not say anything, but nothing was stopping her.

She had told her dad that she might call Mia Munson. Now she did, much to Mia's surprise. The NewsNow anchor agreed to meet with her, and actually seemed eager to do so. They met for lunch on Saturday. And they had a very long, very interesting conversation. When they parted Mia had copies of the same pages that Debra did. She was not thinking about marriage nearly as much as she was thinking about the promotion that would soon be hers.

◆◆◆

Jim Wooten stood in his sunroom, looking out at the water. The movers had just left with the rest of his furniture. The house seemed almost cavernous now that it was devoid of furnishings. That hippy looking older guy had just gone out the front of his ski and taken another crash. The blond headed kid and the other man were helping him in the boat. Jim was going to miss the lake, but he knew there were worse places to retire to than Brazil. With the money he had socked away over the years and his retirement package, he would live very well. The money from this house was nice too. The value of the house had appreciated to over a million and a half dollars since he had built it. But he had not sold it. The banks were offering one hundred percent home equity loans and he had simply borrowed all it was worth. He looked at it as a creative way to sell your home without having to pay a real estate agent, have a home inspection or pay closing costs. On a house of this value, those fees would easily amount to over a hundred thousand dollars. Besides, there was no telling how long it would take to sell a house as big and expensive as his. He had no intention of paying the loan. They would just foreclose in a few months. He was sure HUD had insured the loan, so they could just add this house to their portfolio. One hundred percent financing. How could the government be that dumb?

His only regret was giving up the power he had enjoyed. But, he knew it would not take too long to establish himself in Brazil. He had money, and he knew how to use it. He had cashed in his 401k at an all time high, and, of course, would pay no tax on it. Everything he owned, which was considerable, was now outside the United States, so there would be nothing for the IRS to attach.

There had been none of the planned publicity about Cold-X, and Condor would have to go through the entire approval process. The company had supplied the government with plenty of pills to eradicate the disease, as part of his deal. This was taking place quietly and behind the scene. China was very grateful for the help and apparently had no clue about what had caused the disease to begin with. At some point in time a cure for SARS would be quietly announced, and Condor would get its approval for Cold-X.

His vehicle was being shipped with his furniture, so he took a cab to Tara Field for his chartered flight. He did not have a television or he might have been able to see that good-looking redhead from NewsNow, as she gave the teaser about a big story concerning a local pharmaceutical company, "...coming up right after this break, weather and traffic."

THE END

FROM THE AUTHOR

I have had many ideas over the years for what I was sure would be a good book, and never did anything about it. The idea for this book came one morning when I was working out, while watching the news and the coverage of the SARS virus. I decided that *this* time, I would actually write the book. As my brother, Howe, said, "You have to start by putting words on the page". And so began the process. It took me about four months to write the book and another six to massage it and edit it. What a wonderful experience! You cannot imagine. Sometimes I would read back over a section and wonder, "where did that come from?"

Before going into the real estate management and re-development business over twenty-five years ago, I worked for the U.S. General Accounting Office at the NASA Space Center at Redstone Arsenal, Huntsville, Alabama. I became part of a team evaluating the feasibility of a large space telescope. You may know it as the Hubble Telescope. I had no idea how I would accomplish this task, until a project manager showed me a copy of the weekly progress report. I went on to review various parts of the United States Ballistic Missile Defense Program. The weekly progress report was always important in understanding the programs. In <u>FATAL HEALING</u> a similar project report sets the stage for unraveling the plan of a pharmaceutical company to start a disease for which it already had the cure.

I hope you enjoy it.

For more information on <u>FATAL HEALING</u>
or on the books and services of
HIGHER GROUND STUDIOS,
contact us at:
www.highergroundstudios.com
or call
1-800-430-9708

For <u>FATAL HEALING</u> orders:
www.fatalhealing.com
or call
1-800-430-9710

Printed in the United States
28124LVS00005B/1-42